FINGERTIP FIREPOWER

PEN GUNS, KNIVES, AND BOMBS

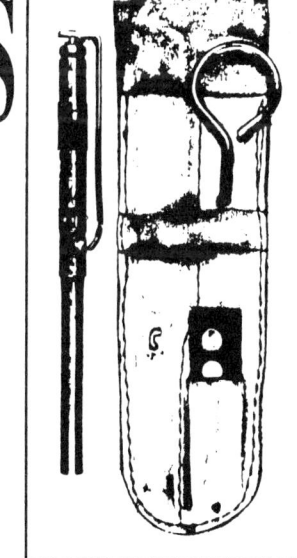

JOHN MINNERY

PALADIN PRESS
BOULDER, COLORADO

Also by John Minnery:

CIA Catalog of Clandestine Weapons, Tools, and Gadgets

How To Kill, Volumes I – VI

Pick Guns: Lock Picking for Spies, Cops, and Locksmiths

Fingertip Firepower:
Pen Guns, Knives, and Bombs
by John Minnery
Copyright © 1990 by John Minnery

ISBN 0-87364-560-X
Printed in the United States of America

Published by Paladin Press, a division of
Paladin Enterprises, Inc., P.O. Box 1307,
Boulder, Colorado 80306, USA.
(303) 443-7250

Direct inquiries and/or orders to the above address.

All rights reserved. Except for use in a review, no
portion of this book may be reproduced in any form
without the express written permission of the publisher.

Neither the author nor the publisher assumes
any responsibility for the use or misuse of
information contained in this book.

CONTENTS

Introduction / 1

The Pen as a Weapon / 3

Pen Knives / 7

Suck and Blow Pen Weapons / 19

Pen Guns / 29

Pen Bombs and Mines / 77

Special Spy Weapons / 85

Inventions Relating to Pen Weapons / 113

ACKNOWLEDGMENTS

The author wishes to express his gratitude to the many people and organizations who assisted in the preparation of this book. Special mention must be made of Mr. H. Keith Melton, Curator, Clandestine Services Museum (private), who gave unstintingly of his photos and documents for this work and deserves a great deal of credit for his efforts and his past kindness.

In Australia:
Mr. Neil Parker, firearms writer, Queensland.
Mr. Ian Skennerton, firearms writer, N.S.W.

In Canada:
Mr. V.K. (Jack) Krcma, forensic firearms examiner, Toronto, Ontario.
Mr. Kurt Willi Krauss, gunsmith, Halton Hills, Ontario.
Mr. Rick Pickering, knifemaker, Brantford, Ontario.
Mr. Joe M. Ramos, firearms writer and illustrator, Scarborough, Ontario.

Mr. Tony Veldkamp, firearms mechanic, Cainsville, Ontario. The staff at Art-Ex (especially Chris), Brantford, Ontario.

In Great Britain:
Mr. Herb Woodend, Pattern Room, Enfield Lock, England.
The Cousins of the Old Firm.

In the United States:
Mr. George Fassnacht, firearms examiner, Philadelphia, Pennsylvania.
Mr. Rick Hummell, staff writer, *Kerville Daily Times*, Kerville, Texas.
Mr. Robert Koch, researcher, Long Beach, California.
Mr. Terukazu Miyamoto, Iuka Testing Labs, Detroit, Michigan.
Mr. Herb Montgomery, New Jersey State Police Crime Lab.
Mr. Tom Swearengen, CWO, USMC (Ret.), firearms writer, Burton, South Carolina.

Finally, my wife, Elsie, who proofreads my manuscripts and humors my obsessions.

INTRODUCTION

Before World War II, the fountain pen was the writing instrument of choice for all who could afford one. Indeed, a good pen was as personal an item as a toothbrush but was much more valuable, and therefore was loaned out with reluctance. The ballpoint pen was introduced toward the end of the war. It immediately found favor with bomber crews and fighter pilots since it didn't leak due to altitude and was considerably less bother to use and maintain than a fountain pen. The ballpoint was rather costly when it first became available, however.

Today, with modern production methods and mass marketing, ballpoint pens are often given away as promotions and for advertising. The pen has become so common that it is no longer noticed. Always at your fingertips or in a pocket or purse, it is the very symbol of inoffensiveness. This casual familiarity makes the pen an ideal item to disguise as a weapon.

Fountain pens are making a bit of a comeback with nostalgia fanatics and also with the recent interest in calligraphy. Being of a larger diameter than ballpoints, they have traditionally been the instrument favored by the designers of pen weapons, particular pen guns, as they are thick enough to withstand the pressures of firing a bullet. Felt-tip marker pens often surpass fountain pens in size and so offer even more room for weapon concealment.

The modern pen has been around now for nearly a century. The development of pen weapons closely followed. Now, their story...

CHAPTER ONE
THE PEN AS A WEAPON

"The pen is mightier than the sword..."

This famous and oft quoted statement is from the play *Richelieu, or The Conspiracy* (act 2, scene 2), by the noted Victorian novelist Edward Robert Bulwer-Lytton. The play, written in 1839, was about the life of Cardinal Armand-Jean Richelieu, arch intriguer and master spy of Louis XIII's France. He was also known as the Grey Eminence, a term we still use for those who manipulate power behind the scenes. (Richelieu was also a central figure in the famous novel, *The Three Musketeers*, by Alexandre Dumas.)

The quote, of course, refers to the observation that the written word is more powerful than any weapon. In this study, we're going to take Bulwer-Lytton's statement quite literally and explore weapons that are made out of pens. It might seem that such weapons were made in limited numbers and that few designs exist; after all, how many possible variations can there be? Well, the reality is that in my research I have found so many different types of pen weapons that I can only show examples in various categories rather than providing an exhaustive list of all that have been made.

The word *pen* derives from the root word *pin*, which is a pointed object that can be jabbed to cause injury. A sharpened metal rod with a cap on one end can be concealed in a shirt pocket and, when needed, may be used as a spike or thrown as a dart. Oriental pens are of the brush type and have hollow bamboo handles, which allow for the storage of messages, drugs, poisons, or pointed objects of various design and intent. The western stylus (pens, and their modern substitute, the pencil) is but a miniature sharpened stake that can be used as a weapon as is.

A fountain pen, ballpoint, or pencil can be used as a weapon as either a fist support in punching or in ice pick or hammer-fist fashion, driving the point into an enemy's eyes, throat, and belly. Ballpoints, for example, can be used quite aggressively and should be held in fighting-knife fashion, grasped solidly with the point protruding from between the thumb and forefinger. It is thrust into a soft target and quickly forced home with the heel of the palm. A mundane but lethal combination of pencil and compass might be carried in a nerdy shirt protector that fits in the breast pocket. If the point of any improvised pen weapon should break or shatter, the broken end can be used for scratching and scraping.

Any pen-like instrument can be employed using Japanese yawara or *kashi-no-bo* fighting techniques. These techniques generally follow karate striking points, which are based on acupuncture charts. These vulnerable targets lie along the midline of the body, either down the front, back, or sides of the victim.

Tossing an object at an enemy's eyes is an effective way to create an opening for a follow-up attack. Pulling an individual into the thrust with the opposite hand not only controls the victim but also adds momentum and thus effectiveness to the stab.

The reason for concentrating on techniques utilizing the common pen is because one must be prepared to employ a follow-up attack after firing a pen gun should the weapon fail to incapacitate, misfire, or if the user misses entirely. Likewise, a bladed pen weapon could snap or fail to penetrate completely.

CHAPTER TWO
PEN KNIVES

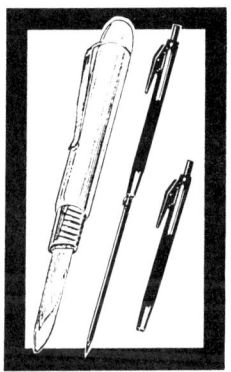

Originally, pen knives were used to repoint the nibs of the old quill pens. They have since become so handy for other uses that they have become synonymous with pocket knives. Here, however, we are concerned with the instrument that is in fact a knife disguised as a pen or other writing instrument.

The most common arrangement is for the "pen" to be in two parts, with the blade concealed inside. One part, usually the cap, forms the hilt or handle of the knife, and the body of the pen acts as the sheath. The unit is generally made of plastic or metal and indeed is often the shell of a commercially available pen. Likewise, the two parts either unscrew, twist off, or pull apart like a regular pen.

The blade is often nothing more than a point or spike. It can be as thin as a lady's hat pin or as thick as a section of reinforcing bar ground to a point. It can also come in the form of a three- or four-sided spike. The advantage of this design, based on a jeweler's

8 / Fingertip Firepower: Pen Guns, Knives, and Bombs

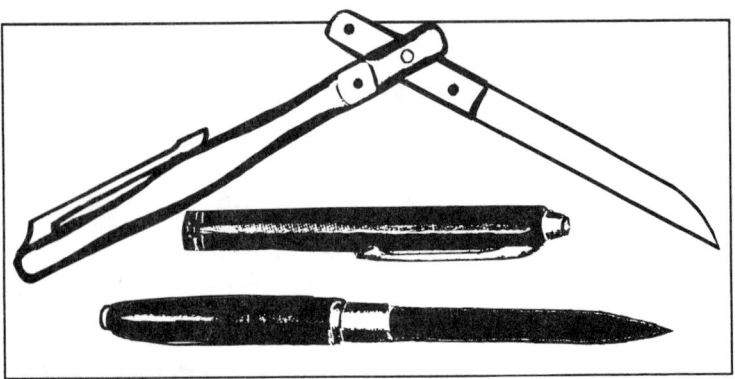

Executive Edge pen knives, sold commercially in the late 1980s. The weapon at bottom is an example of a typical pen knife. (Illustration courtesy of Executive Edge)

scraper and deburring tool, is that it inflicts rather gaping wounds that stay open, encouraging bleeding. Such spikes sometimes have hollowed-out sides with very sharp edges. They can be used to slash as well, and are less subject to breakage than a conventional knife blade.

Such a spiked weapon was put to use in an OSS

Pencil with concealed spike issued by SOE during World War II. "Prechewed" pencils were obtained from English schoolboys. (Photo courtesy of H.K. Melton, Clandestine Services Museum)

design called the Nail and was popular in the China-Burma-India theater during World War II. The British Special Operations Executive (SOE) provided its agents with a spike knife hidden within a scratch pen or chewed-up lead pencil. It was used as an escape and operations aid as well as a weapon. The unit could pry

The SOE Assassin's Needle concealed within a clerk's dip pen. (Illustration courtesy of H.K. Melton, Clandestine Services Museum)

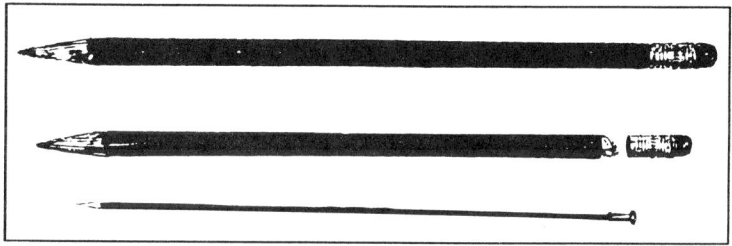

A pencil concealing a sharpened bicycle spoke. (Illustration courtesy of H.K. Melton, Clandestine Services Museum)

back exposed spring latches, gouge spy holes, and pierce gas tanks and tires. It came equipped with a cord-wrapped grip and could be lashed to a stave to make a pike or spear.

The most popular spike pen design in recent years functions like a drafting pencil, with a needle substituting for the pencil lead. The needle is released by thumbing down on the plunger, similar to a ballpoint. It then slides out by gravity—a stop is provided to prevent it from falling out entirely. As with other gravity knives, the business end can be extended by flicking the wrist in time with the releasing operation. Larger drafting pens can contain thicker spikes, of course. A

10 / Fingertip Firepower: Pen Guns, Knives, and Bombs

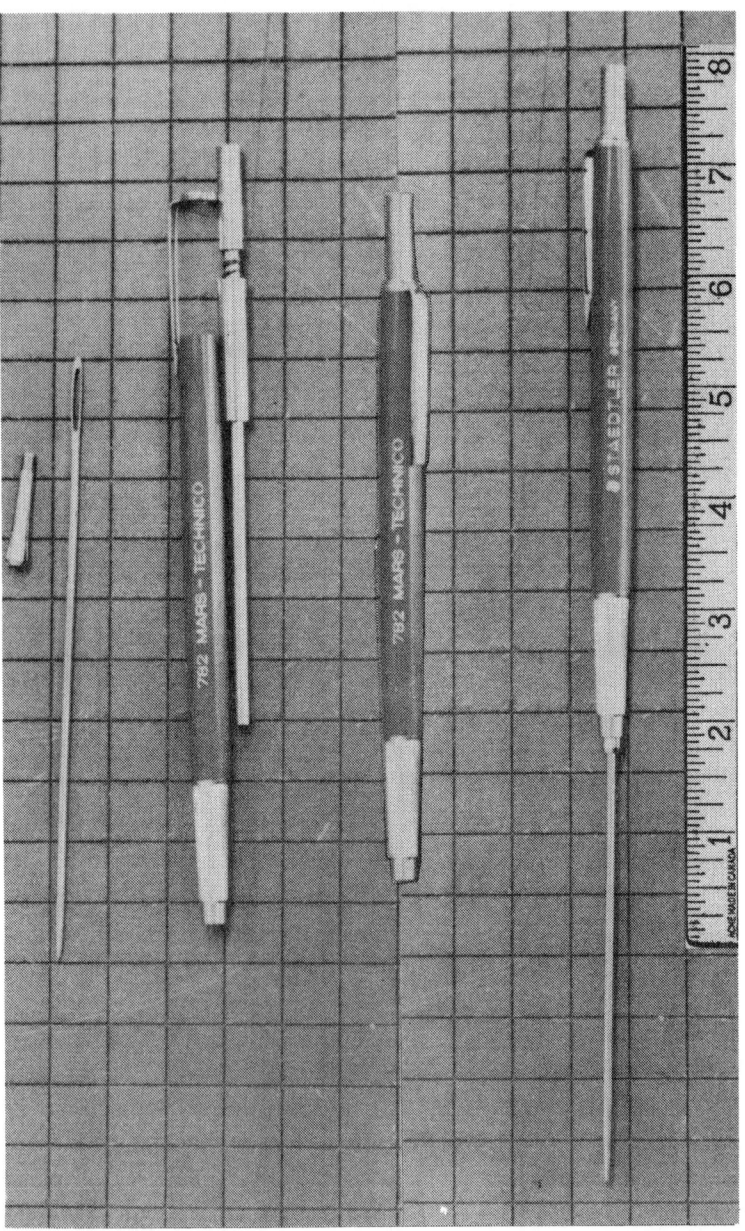

Drafting pencil converted to gravity-operated spike weapon. (Author photo)

similar device, but of slightly different design, is a commercial model called the Guardfather, which is spring-loaded and very powerful.

Pen knives equipped with blades rather than spikes can be used to slice and slash as well as pierce. They come in a variety of designs. I have a commercially produced pen knife by X-ACTO that houses one of their razor-sharp modeling blades. Other pen knives have single- and double-edged blades—some with more blade than handle, others with the opposite arrangement. There are also well-crafted, slim, folding jackknives designed to look like pens.

Perhaps the most popular folding pen knife is one based on the Philippine balisong design. It resembles a ballpoint pen and is commonly made with an aluminum body. The body splits in half along its length and both halves rotate to the rear on individual pivots. One of the halves is jointed with a pocket clip and false plunger assembly, which serves both to lock the halves together through cunning dovetailing and to keep the halves slightly apart, forming a tapering hilt when converted into its knife form.

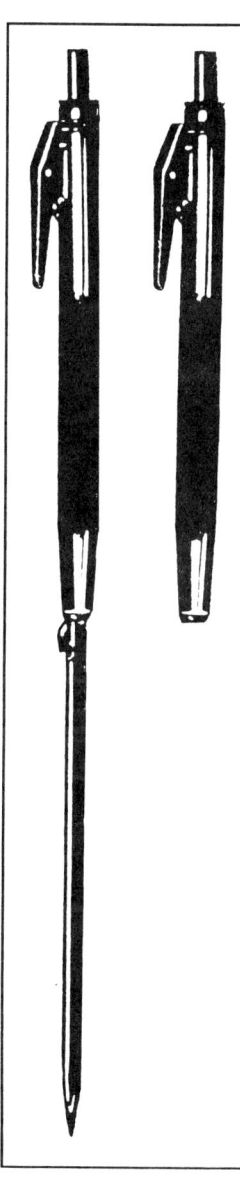

The "Guardfather" spike pen, sold commercially in the 1980s. (Illustration courtesy of Bryg's, Inc)

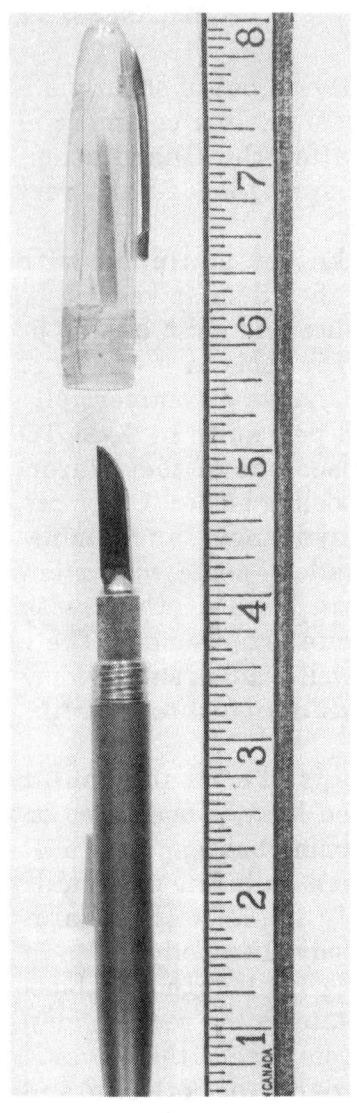

Balisong pen knives are also made with polished brass bodies or are chrome-plated. These heavier types do not have the false plunger (at least the ones I have examined did not). The

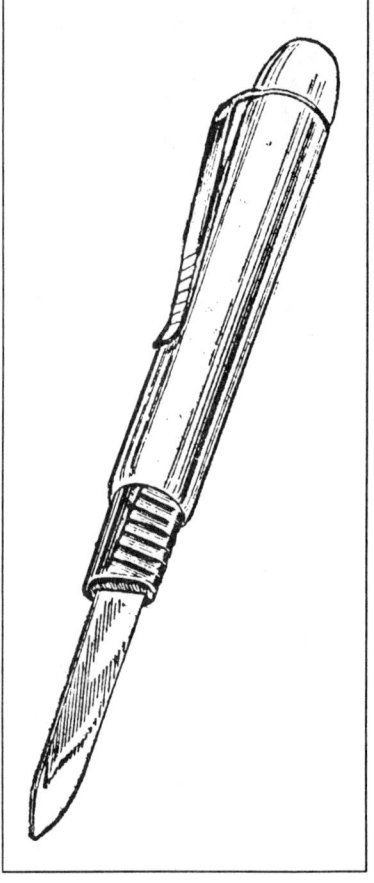

Aluminum-bodied pen knife with clear plastic cap made by X-ACTO. The blade can be replaced with others of different lengths and shapes. A saw-blade version was discovered in a Canadian prison in Manitoba. This knife was sold commercially in the 1970s. (Author photo)

The Hall Penrod pen knife has an aluminum body and a 1 1/2-inch blade. It was sold commercially in the 1950s. (Illustration courtesy of Hall Penrod)

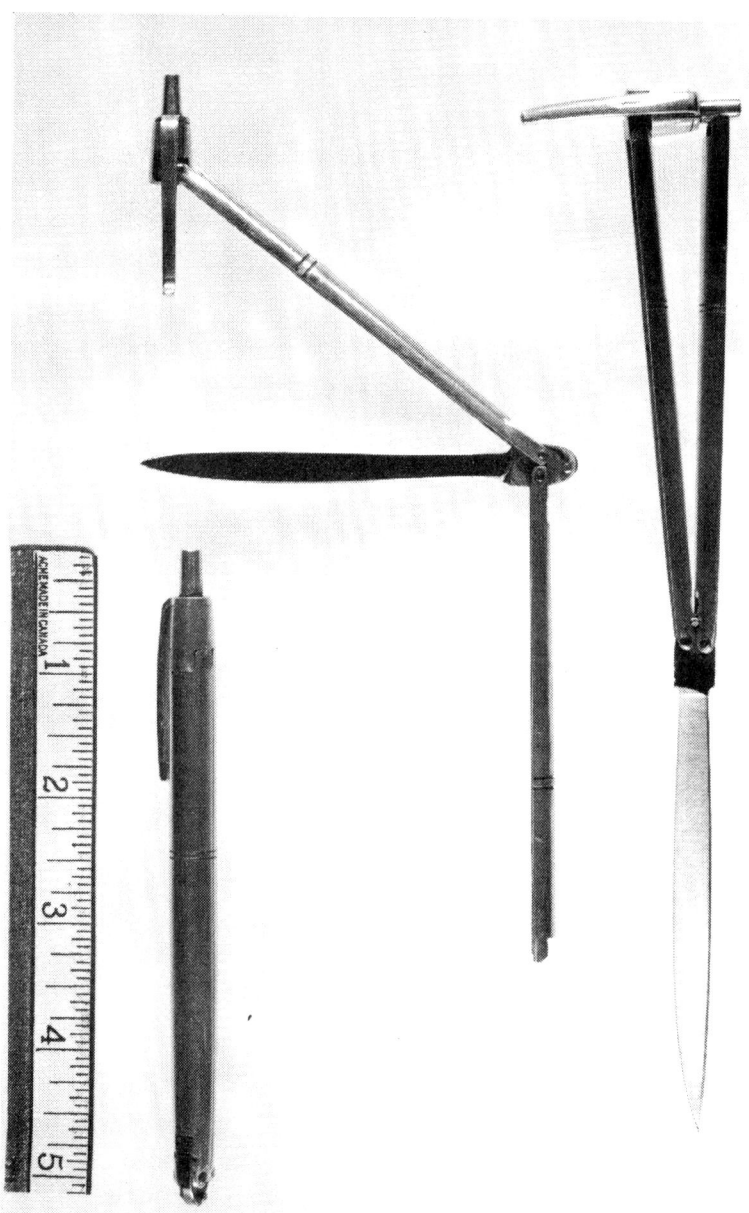

Philippine "Secret Agent" balisong pen knife in different phases of opening. It was sold commercially in the 1960s. (Author photo)

blades are very long compared with other pen knives by virtue of their unique design. They are single edged and roughly triangular shaped. For years they were sold via mail order in the United States by Westbury Sales. I called the company in 1987 and was told that they were no longer selling the item; I gather this was to satisfy the New York City Police Department, although this was not stated.

Johnny Ek Knives also carried a balisong pen knife in its catalog in the late 1960s with the curious proviso: "Not for use within the United States." They are still sold in Manila, of course, where they can be had from the hawkers (after haggling) for the equivalent of $1.50 to $2.00 U.S., or in a department-store sports section for $.90! They've always been a favorite souvenir of servicemen, and during the Vietnam War pilots and aircrews carried them as emergency escape and evasion knives. I recall one being featured in an episode of "The Man From

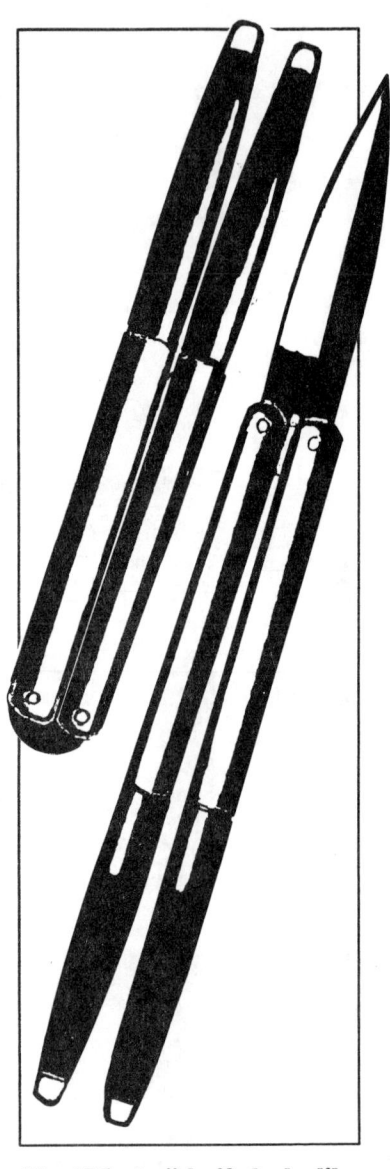

The "Master" knife looks like two pocket pens when folded and works on the balisong principle. It was sold commercially in the 1980s. (Author drawing)

U.N.C.L.E." television series, where it was smuggled into court. Such easy concealment is probably the reason for its disfavor with police.

There is another commercially available balisong pen knife that looks like two pens in a shirt pocket. The unit conceals a rather large blade. When pivoted open, the "pens" form a secure grip.

An improvised pen weapon can be made by grinding and sharpening a section of pen-diameter pipe to the size of a large hypodermic needle, leaving a barbed end. Such knives are targeted in the upper back between the shoulder blades, where the victim cannot extract the knife easily nor staunch the blood flow himself by direct pressure. The open end acts as a conduit for blood flow. Such attacks are best initiated and executed quickly, often before anyone has time to react or even be aware of the assault. The assassin moves on without breaking stride.

It may seem strange, but there are blades specifically designed to snap off inside the victim. These generally are special-purpose assassination weapons. An example of this type of weapon was used in World War II, having a hollow core within the blade that contained poison. A false tip had to be broken off just prior to insertion.

When fighting with conventional edged weapons, it is possible to inflict hand and arm cuts that will incapacitate an opponent, leading to openings to the more vulnerable targets of the throat and torso. This is a luxury that should be avoided when using a pen knife. A pen weapon of any type must be kept concealed until the last possible moment before striking since it depends as much on surprise and shock as it does on wounding effect. It should neither be brandished nor used in a threatening manner, for doing so will put an adversary on guard.

If a pen knife must be drawn for self-defense, it can

be used to prod and cut the assailant enough to dissuade him from continuing the attack, just like a conventional knife (of course there is also a danger of spurring him into a furious rage). Attacking with a pen knife is relegated to assassination techniques, which require pinpoint accuracy and a degree of physiological knowledge regarding where to insert the weapon for lethal results. This is difficult to achieve even with a more powerful weapon. With a pen knife, the best method is to stab repeatedly through the eye sockets into the brain. It is also effective to drive the weapon in up to the hilt and then force it past the hilt onto the pommel. This is the best way to compensate for its short length.

Small, edged weapons such as pen knives must be razor sharp since their effectiveness depends on shock and trauma through blood loss rather than organ damage. The obvious target is the throat and all the major veins and arteries. The user must slash deep, wide, and repeatedly.

As this study deals largely with the use of pen weapons as projectile delivery systems, we can't complete the subject of pen knives without discussing their use as throwing knives. There is a time and a place for everything, but rarely is there an occasion for throwing a weapon and thus disarming oneself. If you *must* throw your weapon, then do so as hard and as fast as possible. Pen knives are so light that you have to make up for what you lack in weight (mass) with increased speed (velocity). Whatever happens, you must be committed to rush in simultaneously with the release of the weapon and immediately drive the point home. Conversely, if your goal is escape, then throw the weapon and run like hell!

Spike pens and pen scribers are the best choices for throwing. Forget about end-over-end circus throwing. Center the knife point forward in the palm of the flattened hand and hold it in place with the thumb. Pull the arm rearward and then shovel the knife at the target with a strong underhand pitch. Release at the trajectory you wish it to take and follow through. A pen knife can be thrown overhand, but there is a greater risk of telegraphing your intentions. Overhand throws are done palm downward, releasing with a downward sweep. Maximum range should be around five feet, depending on the weapon.

CHAPTER THREE
SUCK AND BLOW PEN WEAPONS

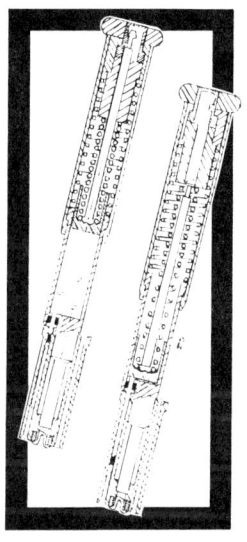

The title of this chapter may sound confusing. What is to be described here are pens that function as syringes and liquid-firing pistols, and others that are miniature blow pipes and air guns.

It doesn't take much imagination to modify a hypodermic syringe to appear as a pen. Just remove the finger flanges, shorten the needle, and paint the body. Added details like a pocket clip and end cap enhance the effect.

What is contained within the syringe is up to the user. Is it to be used for attack or defense? Is the attack to be discreet or blatant? The parameters will determine the load. Some popular examples include heroin, cocaine, methadone, or similar lethal or sublethal narcotic; putrid liquids of decay, HIV-infected blood, or similar biological agents; acids, alkalis, insecticides, or petroleum products to induce toxic shock.

(It is worth noting here that in a voluntary test run on police cadets in Britain, where they were told that

20 / *Fingertip Firepower: Pen Guns, Knives, and Bombs*

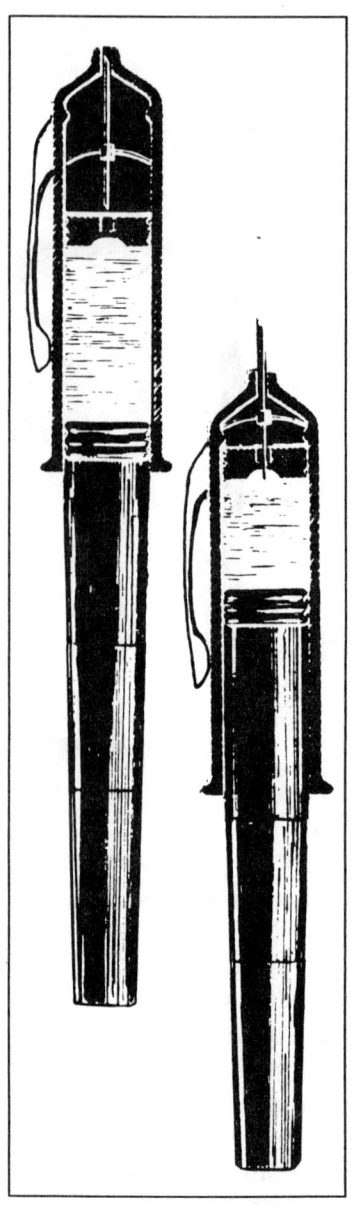

Hypodermic pen based on the Scherer patent. (Illustration courtesy of Scherer)

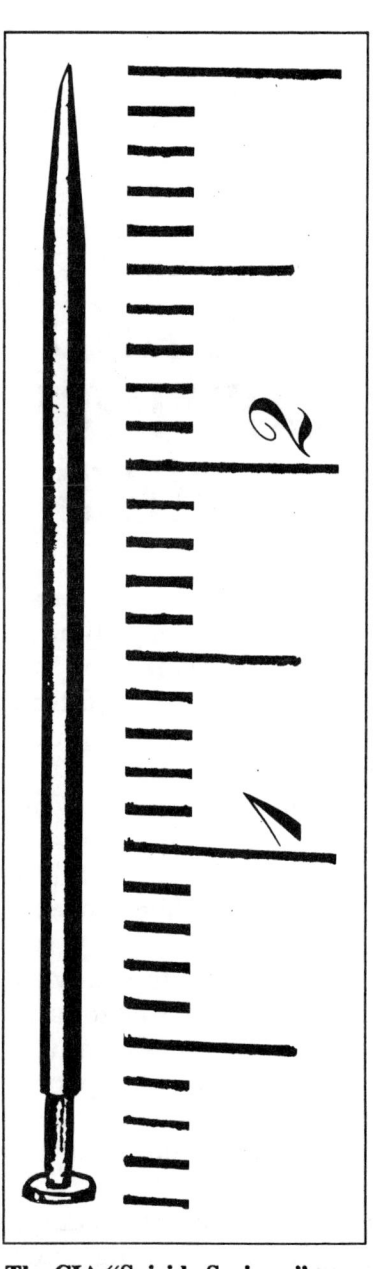

The CIA "Suicide Syringe." (Illustration courtesy of TACC)

sometime during the school day they would be jabbed with a hypodermic needle, over three-quarters of them didn't notice that they had been stuck and thus didn't react to the mock injection.)

Modern fountain pens have an extensible tube that comes out from under the nib, draws ink from a well, and then is retracted. This is accomplished by an ingenious arrangement of threaded members and an internal pump. Honing the tube to hypodermic needle proportions and setting the plunger to expel its reservoir contents create a fine clandestine pen weapon.

Any high-school student knows that hypodermics can also be used at a distance. They make excellent, accurate water (read *liquid*) pistols. Needles come in various gauges and it is possible to tailor the spray to specific needs. For those who don't want to go through the trouble of modifying a syringe, there is a commercially available novelty pen/water pistol that pumps out around ten shots of liquid by depressing the ball-point-like plunger.

Filling the hypodermic pen (or novelty pen) with noxious substances such as acid, lye, or

Remove the cap. Fill in with any kind of liquid such as magic ink or water, etc.

Remove the small cap of the ball pen.

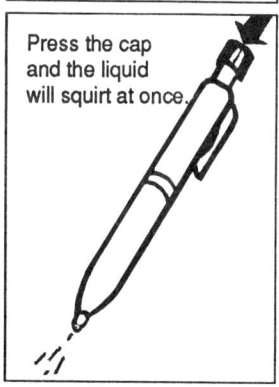
Press the cap and the liquid will squirt at once.

Instruction sheet for a squirting pen gun. (Illustration courtesy of Bob's Novelties)

bleach allows it to be used at ranges beyond arm's length. Gasoline, for example, may be used as an injection agent, face spray, or flame weapon. More exotic loads include cobra venom aimed at the eyes, nose, and mouth. Barry Rothman, an avid herpetologist who once worked for Penguin Industries on their tear-gas pens, designed a felt-tip pen that was filled with boomslang toxin and DMSO (a skin absorption solvent), which could be applied to bare skin anywhere on the body.

Thermometers often come in penlike cases, and a weapon can be handmade from a Pyrex tube gently chisel-sharpened at one end. Filled with a toxic substance, it would be inserted under the skin completely or snapped off at a sufficient depth.

A pen body that has been completely hollowed out can be used as a miniature blowgun. The dart is a pin inserted through a pith ball, which can be blown through the instrument. It is quite accurate at ten to

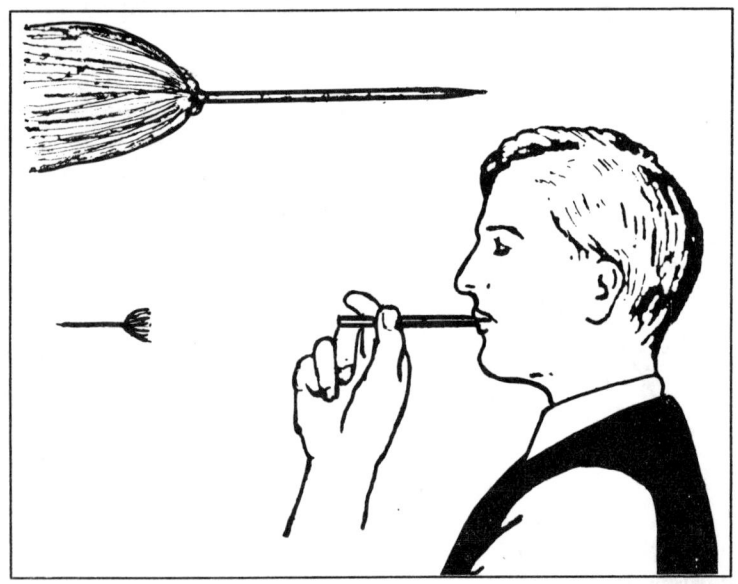

Darning-needle blowgun. (Illustration courtesy of *Popular Mechanics*, 1915)

Suck and Blow Pen Weapons / 23

Exclusive photo of Clayton Hutton surrounded by compasses, silk maps, and escape aids he developed during World War II. Circled is his miniature dart gun that shot phonograph needles. (Photo courtesy of H.K. Melton, Clandestine Services Museum)

twenty feet. Otto Skorzeny, a commando for Adolf Hitler, inspired this device by arming his agents with tubes containing poison darts that resembled cigarettes.

The best of the miniature pen darts using air power was a unit made by Clayton Hutton, who designed escape aids for the British during World War II. They were nothing less than miniature spring air pistols, both single shot and revolvers, that fired tufted phonograph needles.

Pens have even been fashioned into projectiles as large as arrows and spears. A prisoner at Collins Bay Penitentiary in Ontario, Canada, bent on escape, was determined enough to construct his own takedown compound bow from scrap wood and carriage bolts. His arrow was half a dozen Bic pens melted together end to end! The arrowhead was the standard ballpoint cartridge. He was apparently inspired by a television commercial shown a few years back where a character loads a pen into his single-shot target rifle and fires it through one inch of solid oak, exclaiming, "and it still keeps writing!" The prisoner was foiled when

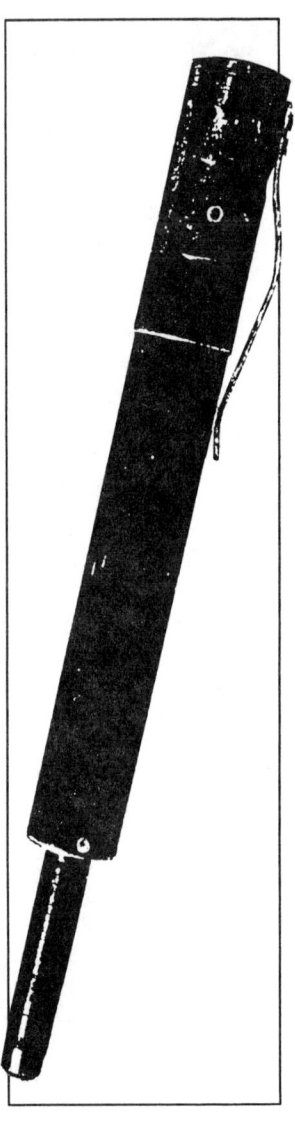

Close-up of Clayton Hutton's dart gun circled in the previous photo. (Illustration courtesy of H.K. Melton, Clandestine Services Museum)

Suck and Blow Pen Weapons / 25

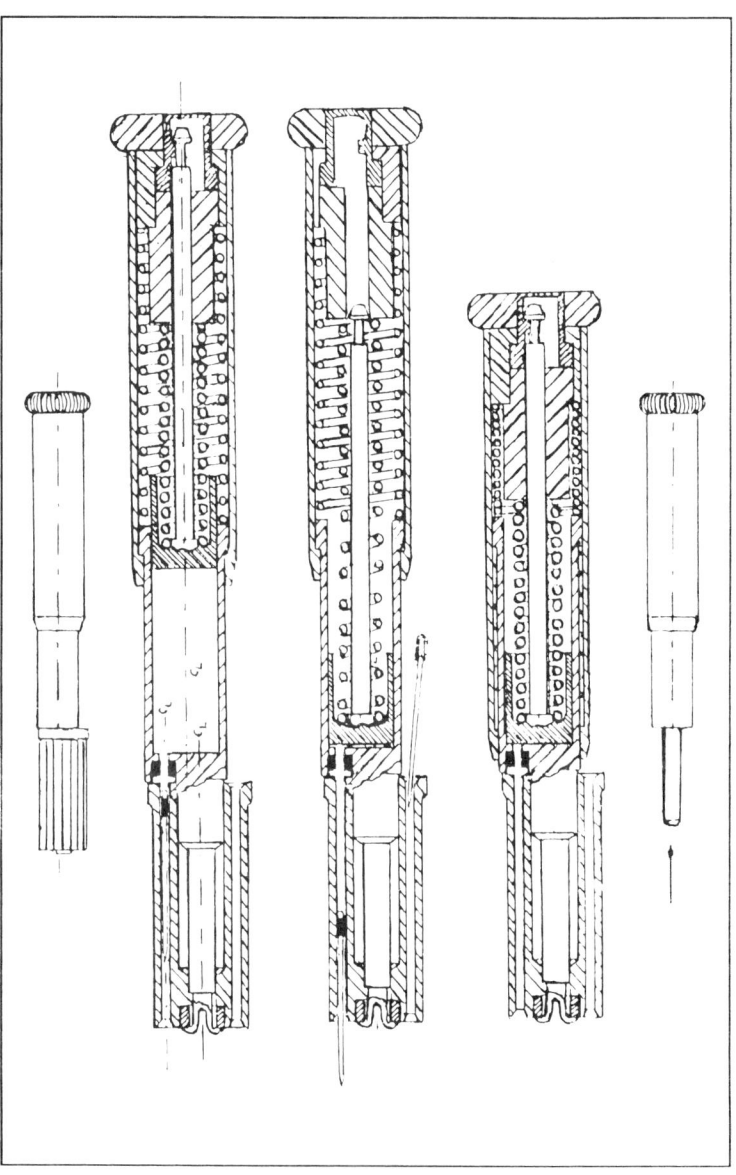

Loading and firing sequences for Clayton Hutton's phonograph-needle dart gun. Illustrated here is the first version of this weapon, a fifteen-shot revolver. It was reportedly used by a French resistance cell during World War II. (Author drawing)

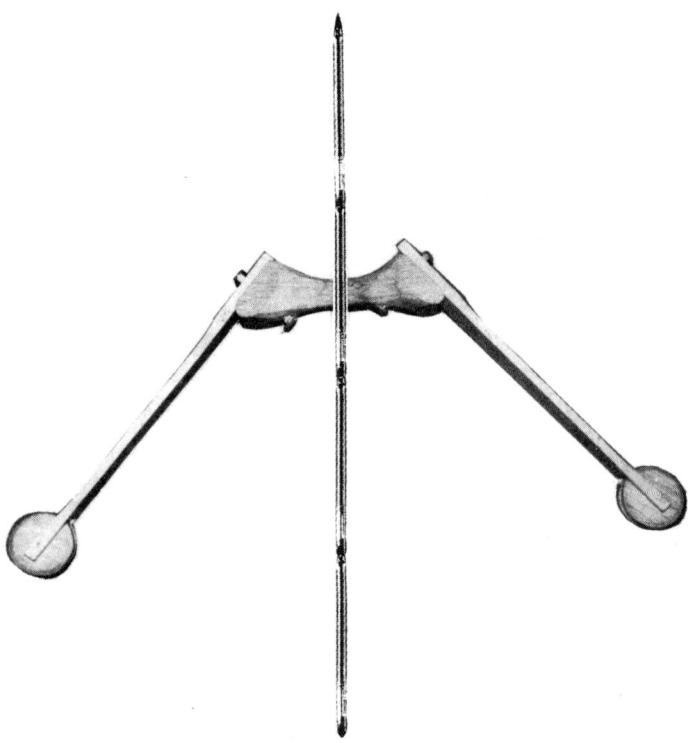

A takedown compound bow made in prison. It used connected pens for an arrow. (Photo courtesy of John Tighe, Correctional Staff College, Kingston, Canada)

the weapon was found during a search for contraband drugs.

Telescopic pen pointers favored by lecturers can be used as arrows for rubber catapult devices. They are fired backwards (i.e., fat-end first), with the pocket clip acting as the hook that connects to the nocking point on the bowstring. The blunt end is replaced with or fashioned into a conical point.

Though it would require some effort, the telescoping sections of a pen pointer could be designed to lock into place to form a rigid épée-like weapon that could be thrust into an opponent's soft spots. An optional poisoned tip adds to the drama.

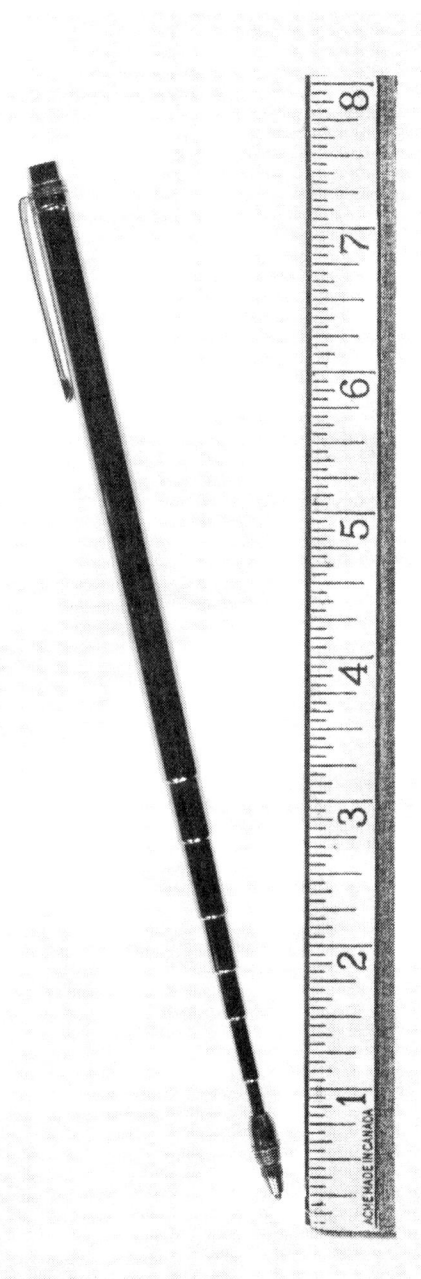

Telescoping pen weapon. (Author photo)

CHAPTER FOUR
PEN GUNS

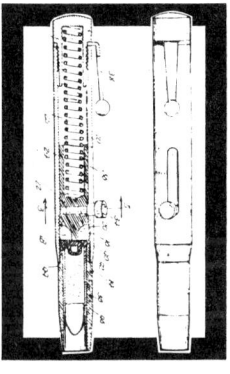

Pen guns do not always fire bullets. They can be loaded with blanks to start races, scare off muggers or dogs, attract help, or command attention. Pen guns can also launch distress flares and starshell rockets. The most common pen gun by far is the tear-gas type, which can also be used to dispense insecticides and room deodorizers.

Pen guns are notorious for their propensity to misfire. The reasons for this are obvious when one considers the relatively small size of the device and the work expected from the moving parts. The coil mainspring will sometimes develop a "set" and lose its springiness, as will all springs when kept compressed for any length of time. This will result in a light blow to the primer of either rimfire or centerfire ammunition, causing a misfire. This is a problem if it occurs with any weapon, of course, but is perhaps more acute when using a pen gun, for it is literally a weapon of last resort.

The chance for a misfire can be diminished by keeping the unit in A-1 shape and test-firing it regularly. A stronger mainspring can be substituted if needed, and experimenting with different brands of ammunition is recommended. European .22-caliber cartridges have thinner cases—therefore the firing pin doesn't have to hit as hard as with American-made ammo. By judiciously thinning the case in the primer area with a fine file (and with all due caution), the chances of a misfire will become more unlikely. Quality target ammunition, with its low record of misfires and moderate velocity, is a good choice for a reliable .22 load in a pen gun.

Pen guns, being the ultimate pocket pistols, are also prone to stoppages caused by lint and other pocket debris. Like a good soldier, the owner should clean and oil his weapon whenever he is preparing to go into situations requiring its use. The pen gun might have to be fired from underneath clothing, so this operation should also be tested before being attempted *in extremis*. Never use a pen gun to intimidate or threaten, since its effectiveness lies in its immediate and surprising use, and *always* consider follow-up techniques after firing one. See Chapter Two on pen knives for information on follow-through.

Percussion Cap Pen Guns

The percussion cap pen gun is the pistol reduced to its basic elements. It is the soul of simplicity. It is essentially an aluminum tube threaded at both ends, each having a percussion-cap nipple onto which a percussion cap fits. Inside there are a coil spring and a sliding steel bolt that impacts against the percussion cap. There is a short longitudinal slot through which a rounded thumbpiece appears, which itself is threaded into the hammer bolt. A plastic pen cap with molded pocket clip slips over either end and does not have to be removed when the gun is fired. The weapon is discharged by pulling back the thumbpiece to full-cock

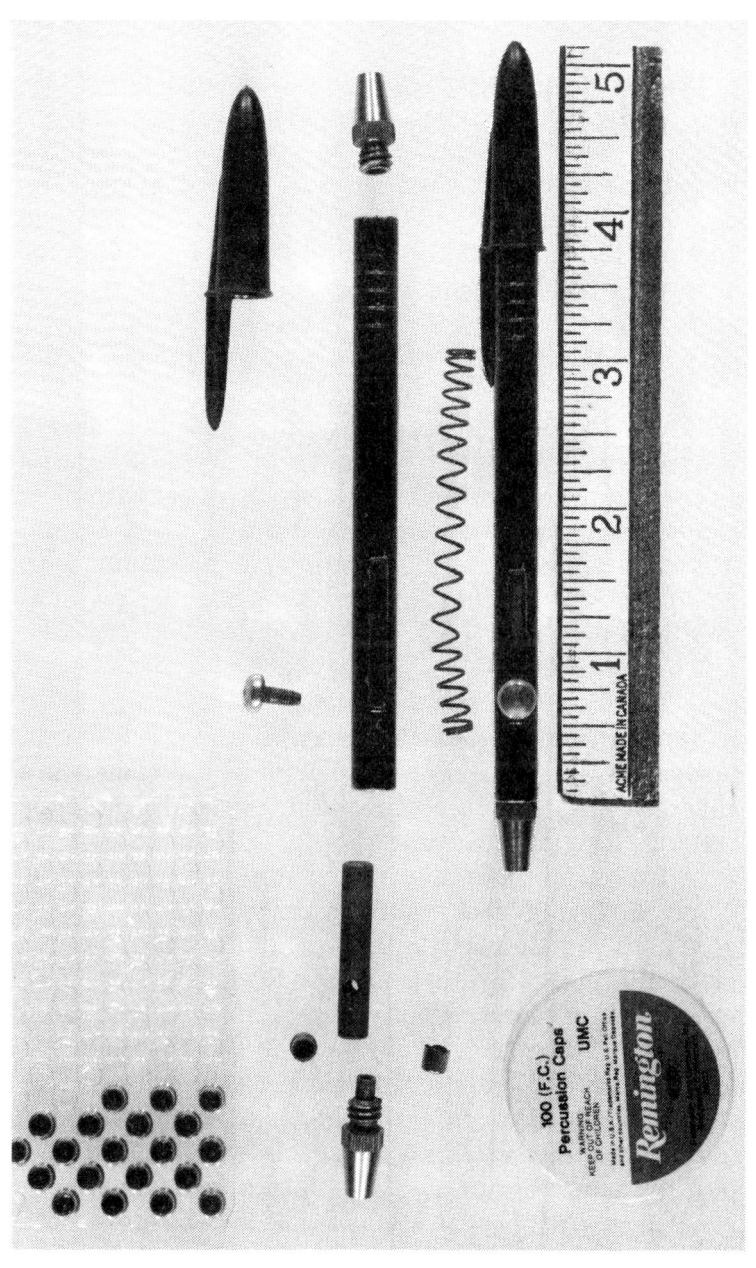

Disassembled percussion-cap pen gun. (Author photo)

and letting go.

These devices were once sold as novelty noisemakers. I bought several at a sports outfitter's establishment for $2.50 each in 1986. They came with a painted lacquer finish in red, green, or blue. They were nothing more than toys—or were they? The percussion nipple on these units could accept and fire percussion caps used with black powder pistols. They could easily fire projectiles.

Plastic percussion caps shoot out an innocuous jet of flame. By carefully cutting out the paper primer retainer, a minuscule amount of fulminate is revealed. By packing the contents of several caps into one, a sure-fire powder igniter is made, even without access to copper percussion caps. By adding a small charge of fffg (triple-fine grain) black powder and topping with an appropriate pellet, a very cheap Stinger pistol is produced.

Pinfire Pen Guns

In the world of arcane weaponry, perhaps the most bizarre is the pinfire pen gun. Pinfire firearms were the weapons of choice in mid-nineteenth century Europe. Though they were never embraced by the military, they were popular for sporting and self-defense, particularly in France and Belgium.

The firing pin is contained within the cartridge and rests in a cup of priming powder made up of a fulminate mixture, which itself rests within the propellant powder. The cartridge may appear crude to modern eyes, but at the time it was quite an advance in cartridge design. Pinfire cartridges are still used today but at a rapidly declining rate, chiefly by collectors of pinfire firearms who want to maintain the tradition.

The weapon presented on the facing page was designed by Sergio Biason of the Philippines. The commercial fountain pen serves only as a disguise and han-

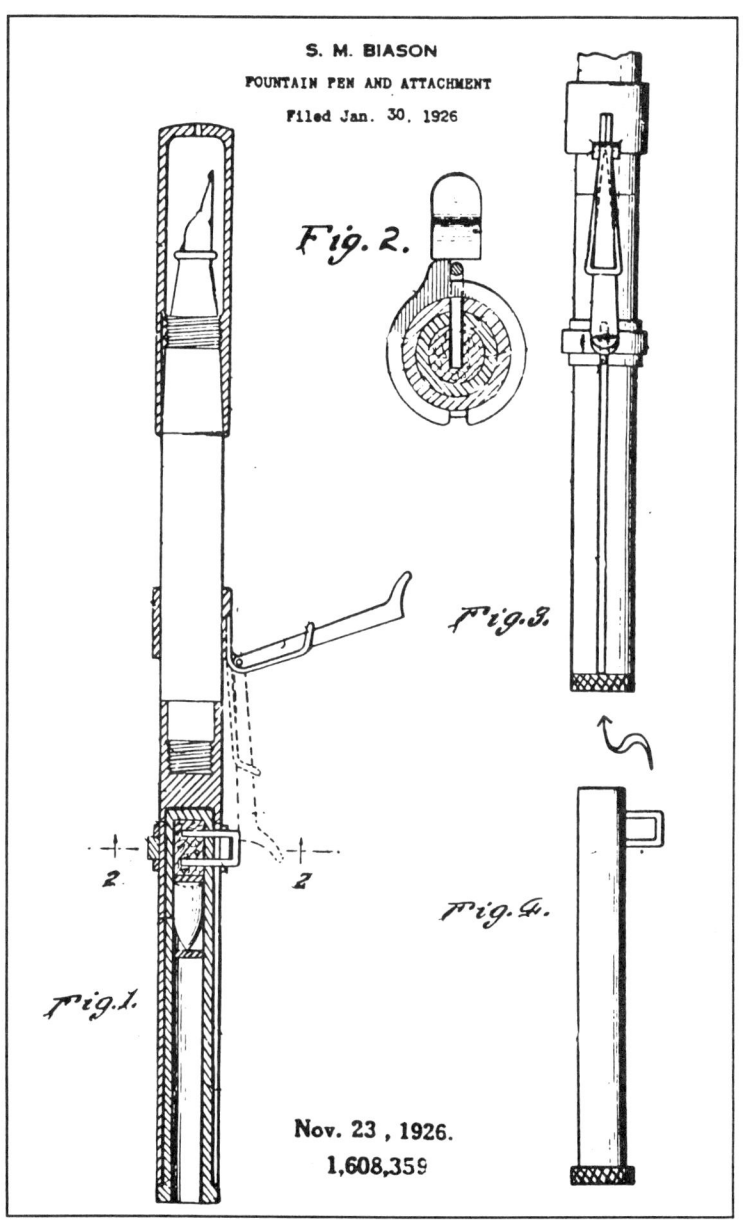

A pinfire pen gun made from a fountain pen by S.M. Biason. (Author redrawing of Biason patent)

dle for his device, which screws onto the butt of the pen. The trigger is a slip hammer that is drawn back like a mousetrap and released, striking the staple-like firing pins.

In the Philippines, there are legal strictures and financial binds on citizens who want to reload ammunition. Cartridges are often reloaded with matchhead compositions and scrapings from toy caps. The fact that they reload primers is interesting, as it is an activity never indulged in by more industrialized societies, where primers are very cheap.

(If reloading cartridge primers sounds desperate, then consider what Siberian hunters must do to reload .22s. They reprime the rims with matchhead paste and fabricate tools for removing the indent from the fired case. Percussion caps are treated in a similar manner—the composition is held in cups made from aluminum foil and pinched in place.)

The barrel of Biason's weapon also serves as a cartridge case. The bullet is inserted against a wad over the powder (typically composed of ground-up match heads) and another wad is used to hold it in place. A safety

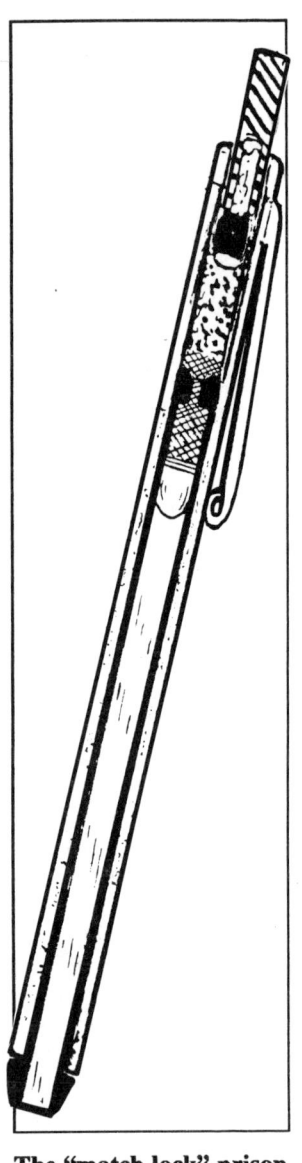

The "match lock" prison pen gun. It is fired via a match head within an abrasive liner. (Author drawing)

ring keeps the hammer away from the firing pins until it is rotated to fire position. To reload, the used barrel is slipped from its slotted tubular housing and a new one is inserted in its place.

This particular weapon is significant not only because of its design but also as an example of clever improvisation. It reflects the ability to make a weapon from any available material using original techniques.

Prisoners have also used match heads to fire-off guns and explosive devices. A "match lock" pen gun manufactured in prison is based on such a miniature explosive device. The charge is initiated by a match pulled or pushed along a rolled-up friction card.

Needlefire Pen Guns

Needlefire cartridges are even more obscure than pinfire cartridges. Their heyday was during the Franco-Prussian War, when the Dryse needlefire bolt-action rifle revolutionized the military firearms of Europe and prompted the shift to bolt-action arms, which was to last

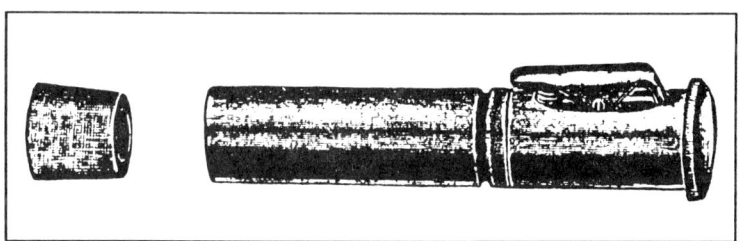

Needlefire detonating-cork pen gun used in the 1890s. (Illustration courtesy of Knallfix)

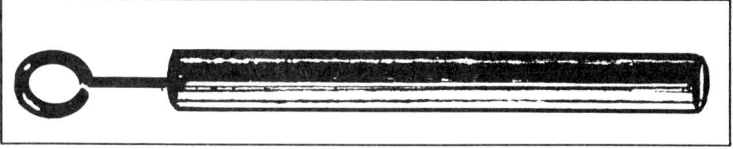

Economy version of the detonating-cork pen gun (c. 1900). This pull-release system was the forerunner of today's zip guns. (Illustration courtesy of Knallfix)

36 / Fingertip Firepower: Pen Guns, Knives, and Bombs

A turn-of-the-century woodcut advertising Knallfix guns being used to scare off a pack of dogs. (Illustration courtesy of Knallfix)

Detonating-cork "machine gun." This firing system can be applied with other pen guns. (Illustration courtesy of Poyet)

for nearly a century.

The needlefire system was utilized in detonating cork guns that were used on stage as prop weapons, as alarm guns, and for amusement as noisemakers. The detonating cork was essentially a hollowed-out cork that contained a fulminate and gunpowder mix in the tapered end. When a needlelike firing pin was driven into the mixture by a released coil spring, it discharged with a satisfying bang and pall of smoke. The cork was blown into harmless bits. These cork guns could be made more dangerous by whittling the cork to allow it to seat deeper within the barrel. A projectile or shot charge was then inserted over the cork, to be fired upon discharge.

The detonating-cork pen gun seems to be the earliest example of a penlike firearm. It presages "L-slot" pen guns, pull-release zip guns, and the CIA Stinger weapons. There was even a battery arrangement of detonating-cork pen guns that would fire like a machine gun!

Rimfire Pen Guns

Pen guns in .22 caliber are preeminent, and the ideal cartridge for the pen-gun format is the widely available .22 rimfire. It is generally safe to fire in all but the flimsiest of zip guns and is small enough to be fitted into even pencil-slim designs, yet the round is capable of inflicting stinging to lethal wounds in defensive or offensive undertakings.

The earliest record of a rimfire pen gun that I could find was the Frederick S. Cocho patent of 1928. It is an elegant design incorporating all the best features of a .22 pen gun. By referring to the patent drawings, one can see this weapon's simplicity, strength, and facility of operation. It has a long barrel, strong breech, and well-designed striker bolt. The pocket clip serves as the trigger, which initiated a theme for pen guns. It might appear to be rather

38 / Fingertip Firepower: Pen Guns, Knives, and Bombs

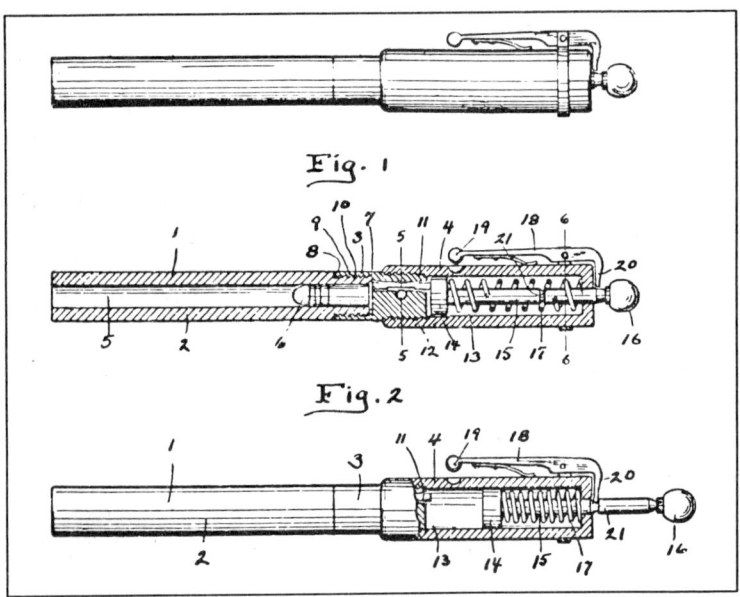

The earliest reference to a true pen gun—the Cocho .22-caliber pen gun. (Author redrawing of Cocho patent)

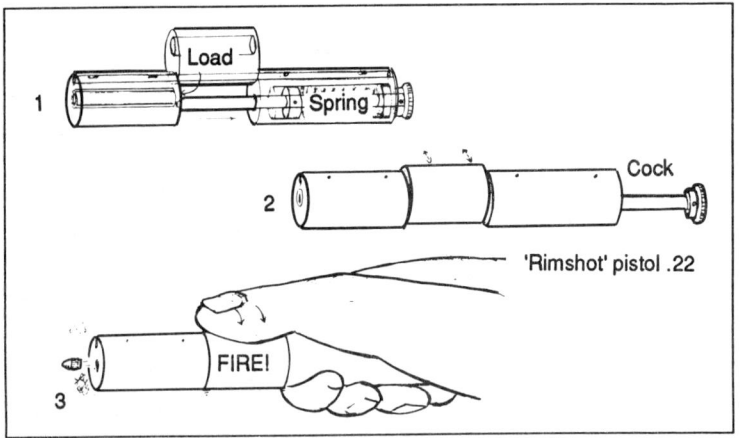

The .22-caliber "Rimshot" pistol. The body is made from three sections of wooden broomstick. The middle section swings up for loading after the striker is drawn back. Once loaded, the user presses the middle section closed, which aligns the striker and fires the weapon. (Author drawing)

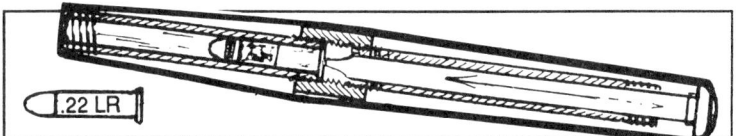

Zip pen gun utilizing elastic band. To fire, the user pulls back on the carriage bolt and releases. The .22 LR bullet breaks the elastic band upon discharge. (Author drawing)

large, but the weapon conformed to the dimensions of fountain pens of that period.

The .22-caliber weapons of the British Secret Service and SOE and American OSS and CIA, as well as the zip guns illustrated in this section, all can be loaded with various special .22 rounds. Some exotic rounds are:

1. *Solid gold bullets* (OSS). Heavier than lead, they hit comparatively harder, compensating for the reduced velocity of a Stinger pistol or silenced round. Today, depleted uranium can be considered, having the added advantage of being pyrophoric.

2. *Explosive rounds.* Explosive rounds such as Velex/Velet bullets enhance wounding effects when striking dense tissue. Barry Rothman designed an explosive bullet for soft targets (e.g., the stomach) that worked on fuse delay rather than impact initiation.

3. *Poison bullets.* These are made by hollowing out mushroom ammo and filling with cyanide, strychnine, or biotoxins.

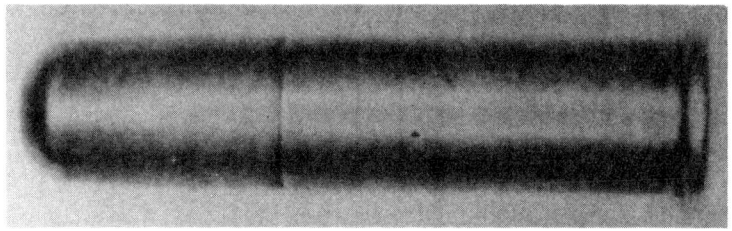

A .22-caliber time-delay exploding bullet developed by Barry Rothman. The round was used in pen guns and the Venus double-barreled submachine gun tested by CIA. (Author photo)

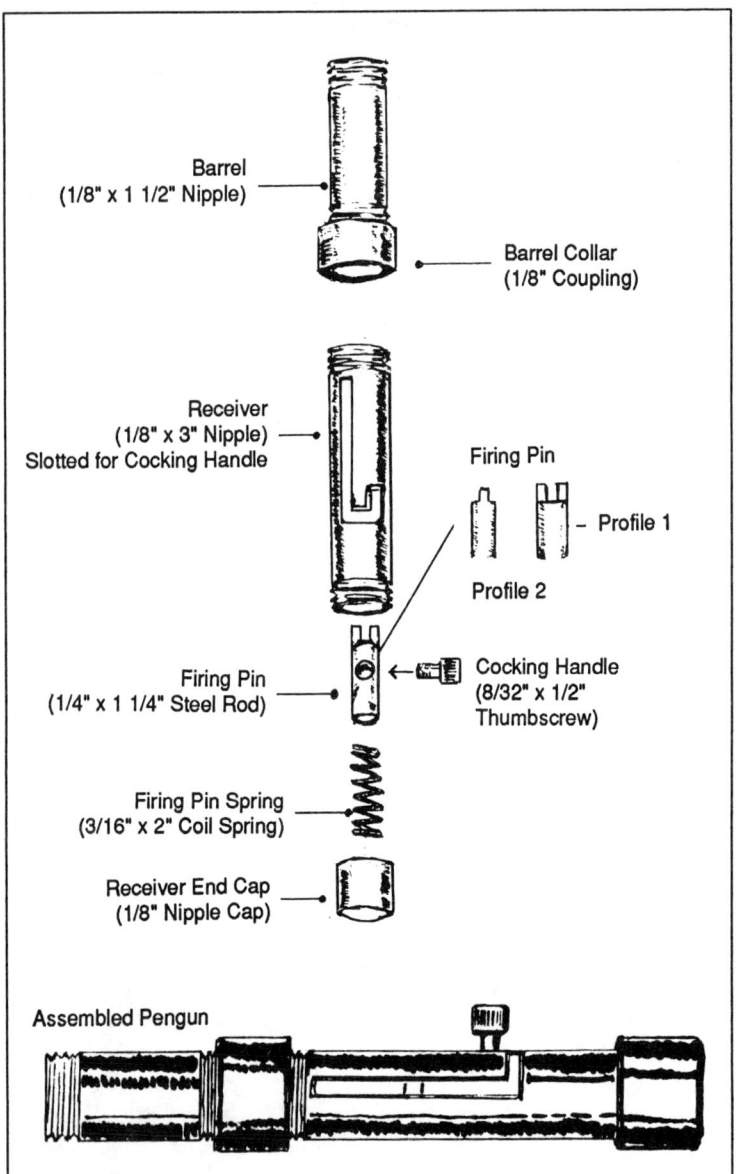

A .22 pen gun made from common materials. This broadside was circulated at gun shows and meetings to demonstrate the futility of firearms legislation. (Illustration courtesy of Bruce Hamilton)

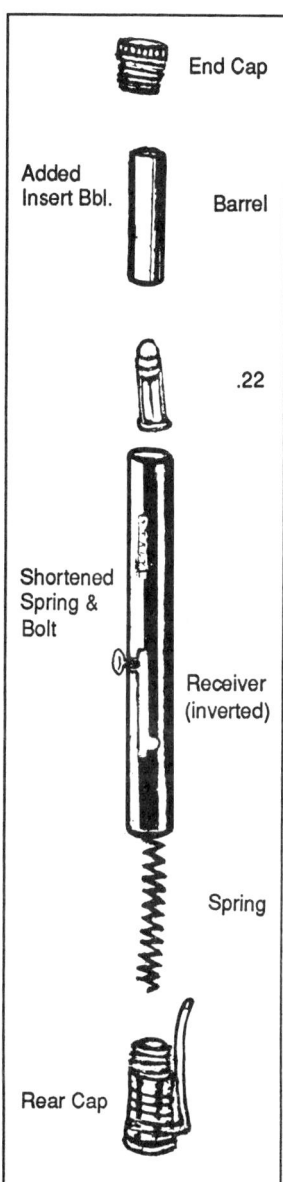

A .22 blank gun conversion requiring simple modifications. (Author drawing)

4. *Metal-jacketed .22 bullets.* These were issued to comply with The Hague Rules of War, which banned lead bullets. Stingers, silenced pistols, and survival rifles (used by American units such as the Jedburgh teams that operated in occupied Europe during World War II) were made to comply to The Hague's restrictions by using this round.

5. *Industrial blanks.* Used to propel oversized projectiles such as flares, darts, or small arrows, these are regular blanks that have been modified by epoxying .177 or .22 BBs or pellets to their crimps. They are best used with very small pen guns or with designs that lack the breech support for safe firing with standard ammunition. Modified industrial blanks also allow for test firing without straining a weapon and shortening its lifetime. They are actually sublethal under most conditions and are perhaps best suited for use as a Stinger cartridge.

In regard to disguising pen guns, it is worth mentioning at this point that although some units have pencil-tip or ballpoint inserts, most of the pistols sport barrels that are rather obvious to even casual observers. This shortcoming can be overcome by the insertion of a tampion made from a pencil stub whittled down to friction fit into the bore. A ballpoint insert will serve equally well. It is wise to remove the tampion before firing, but little harm would result if it were fired out along with the bullet, especially at the ranges that pen guns are nor-

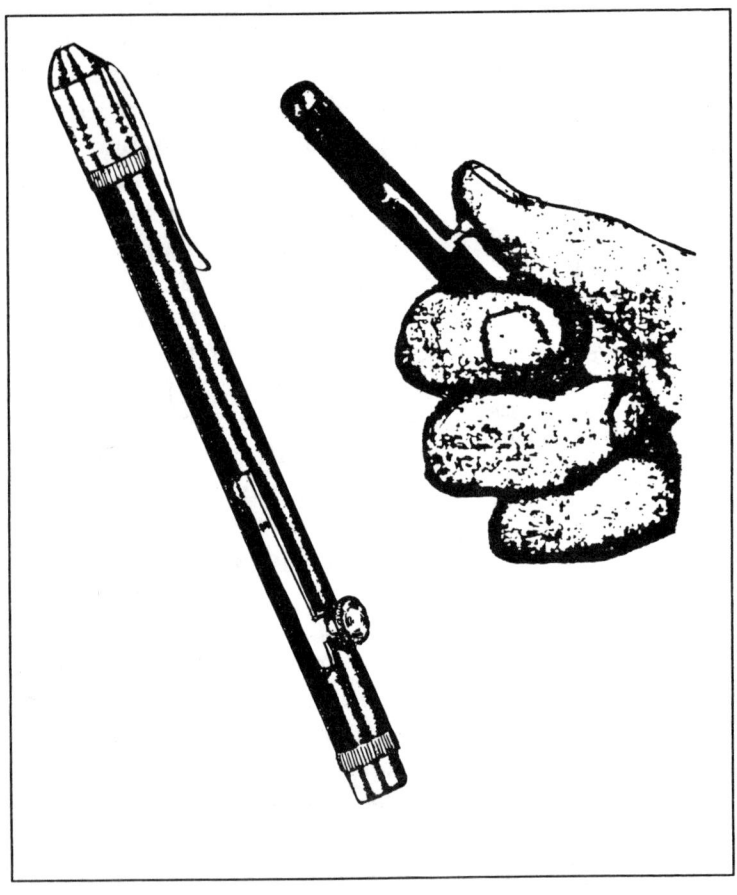

A short-lived advertisement of Merchanteers Inc. .22-caliber ballpoint gun. It was a real pistol, not a blank gun, and sold by mail order for $4.95 in the early 1960s. The weapons were seized from Merchanteers in police raids. (Illustration courtesy of Merchanteers)

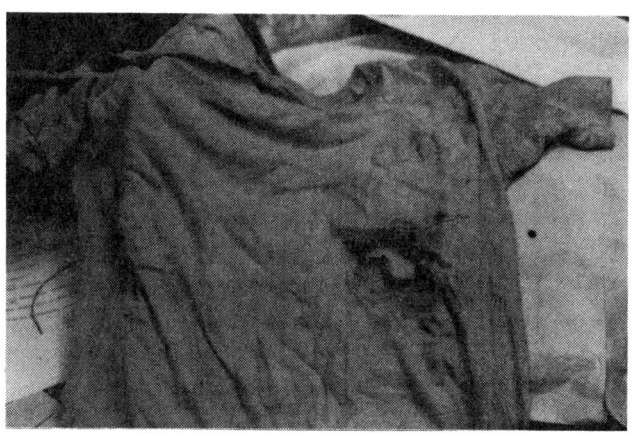
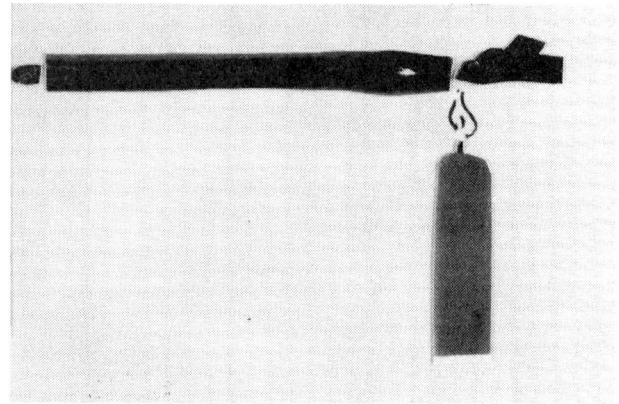

Evidence photos of an attempted suicide. The victim inserted a cartridge in a pipe and held it over a candle. The T-shirt shows the result. This is a good example of extremely simple weapon creation. (Photo courtesy of Howard Montgomery, New Jersey Crime Lab.)

mally employed. The owner can also paint his pistol red, yellow, white, or a rainbow of colors if need be to further camouflage his weapon.

Two contenders for the simplest firearms that might be classified in dimension, if not description, as pen guns were made from lengths of pipe. In the first case, an individual bent on self-destruction jammed a rifle cartridge into a short length of pipe, held it over a

44 / *Fingertip Firepower: Pen Guns, Knives, and Bombs*

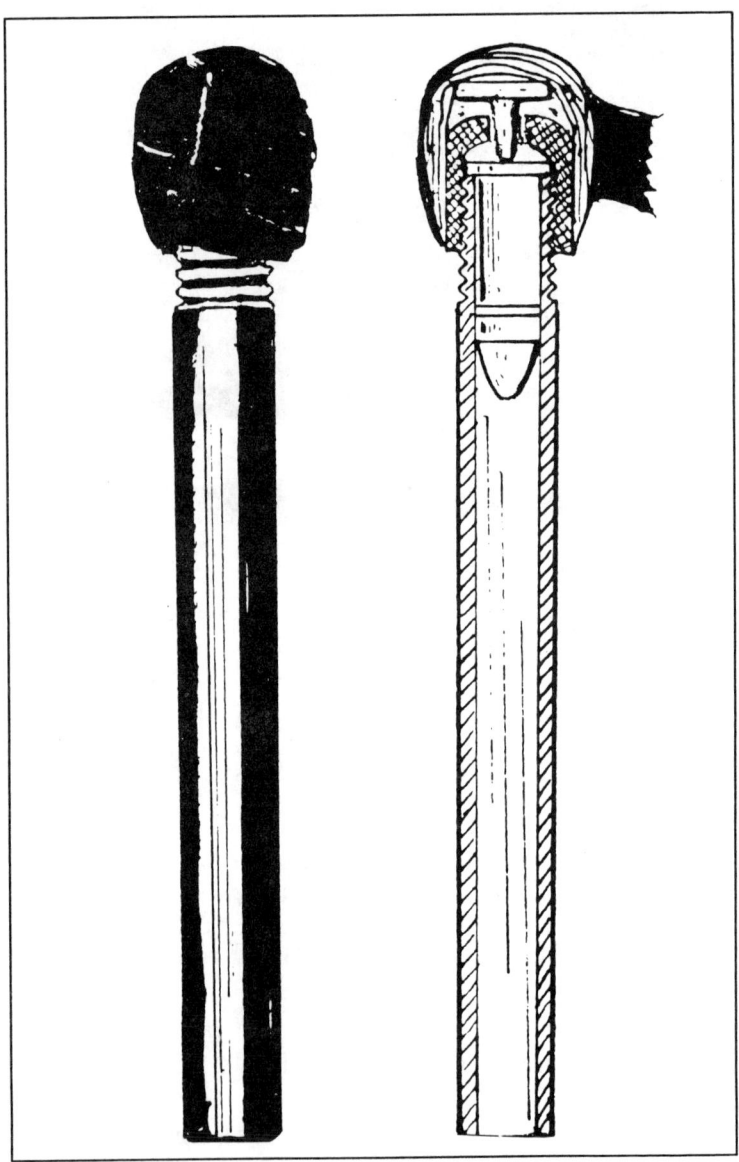

A .38 slap pistol. This extremely simple weapon is made from pipe parts, a roofing nail, and tape. It is grasped solidly in one hand and fired by hitting smartly with the opposite palm. (Author drawing)

candle flame with the muzzle pointed at his heart, and patiently awaited the cook-off of the round, which eventually exploded. The individual survived the suicide attempt only due to his bad aim.

In the second case, a five-inch length of grease nipple extension was set up to accept a .22 round. The demonstrator plonked one in, directed the muzzle at a piece of wood several feet away, and rapped the cartridge base smartly with an eight-ounce ball peen hammer, firing the round. (Don't try this at home, kiddies.) The accuracy of such an arrangement would preclude it from being used as a weapon, though he did hit the board!

(As late as the 1950s, pirates of the South China Sea fired their homemade cannons by means of percussion-cap nipples threaded into the touch holes. After aiming the guns, they were fired by rapping the caps with a short length of iron bar. A percussion pistol could be similarly fired.)

GAMES AND ENTERTAINMENTS

FUN! Just out! Shooting fountain pen, looks like real pen, makes report like pistol, 25c. Two hundred other tricks and puzzles. Send 2c for illustrated catalogues. J. Grandefeld, 1238 Theriot Avenue, Bronx, New York.

BING-Bang Fountain Pen, 30c. Chung Ling Soo's Linking Ring Trick 25c. Mysterious Tumbler and Vanishing Coin 25c. Trick loaded cigars 10c. Bogus Spike 10c. Stage money, 15 bills 10c. Hundreds of others. Send 3c for large catalog. D. DeLuca, Dept. A, 880 Charles St., Marieville, R. I.

An early advertisement for shooting pens (possibly using .32 blanks). (Illustration courtesy of *Popular Mechanics*, 1917)

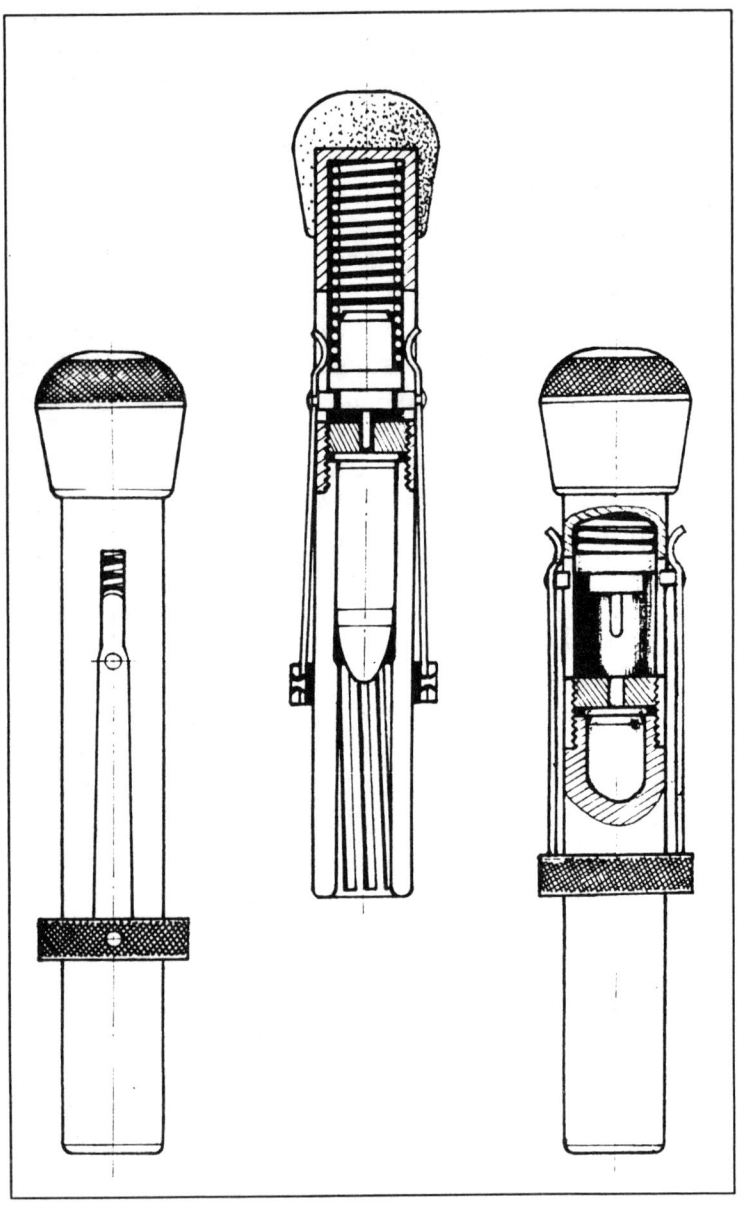

The Webber patent is the earliest centerfire pen gun. The user fires the weapon's .32-caliber bullet by squeezing the ring back towards the base. (Illustration courtesy of Joe Ramos)

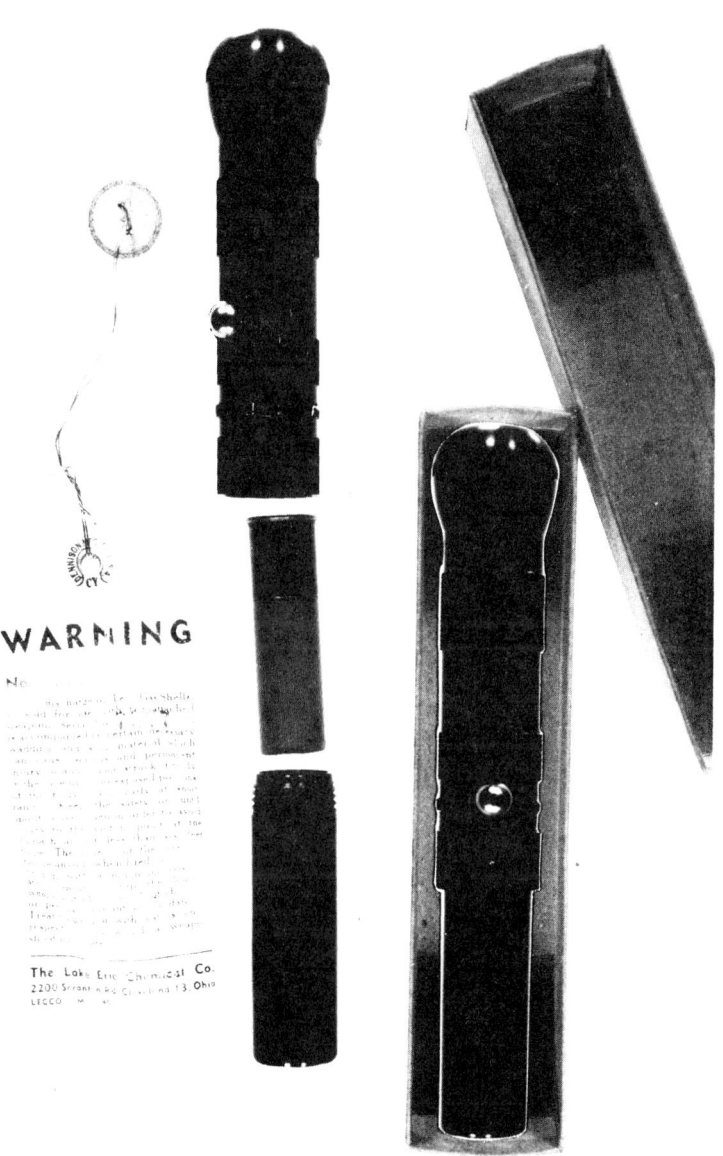

The LECCO 20-gauge tear-gas billy in its box, complete with warning. It is a robust aluminum weapon that incorporates features of the Ailes patent. (Author photo)

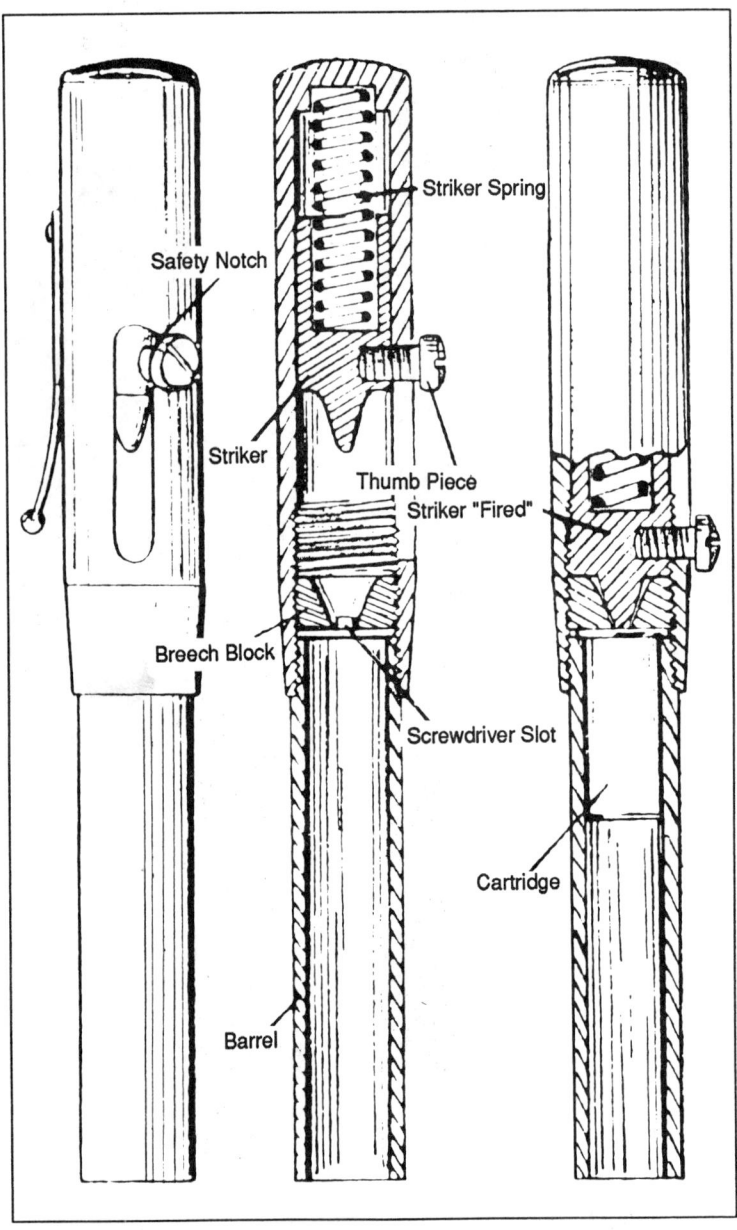

The first tear-gas pen gun, patented by Dr. Byron C. Goss. It could also fire bullets. (Illustration courtesy of Tom Swearengen)

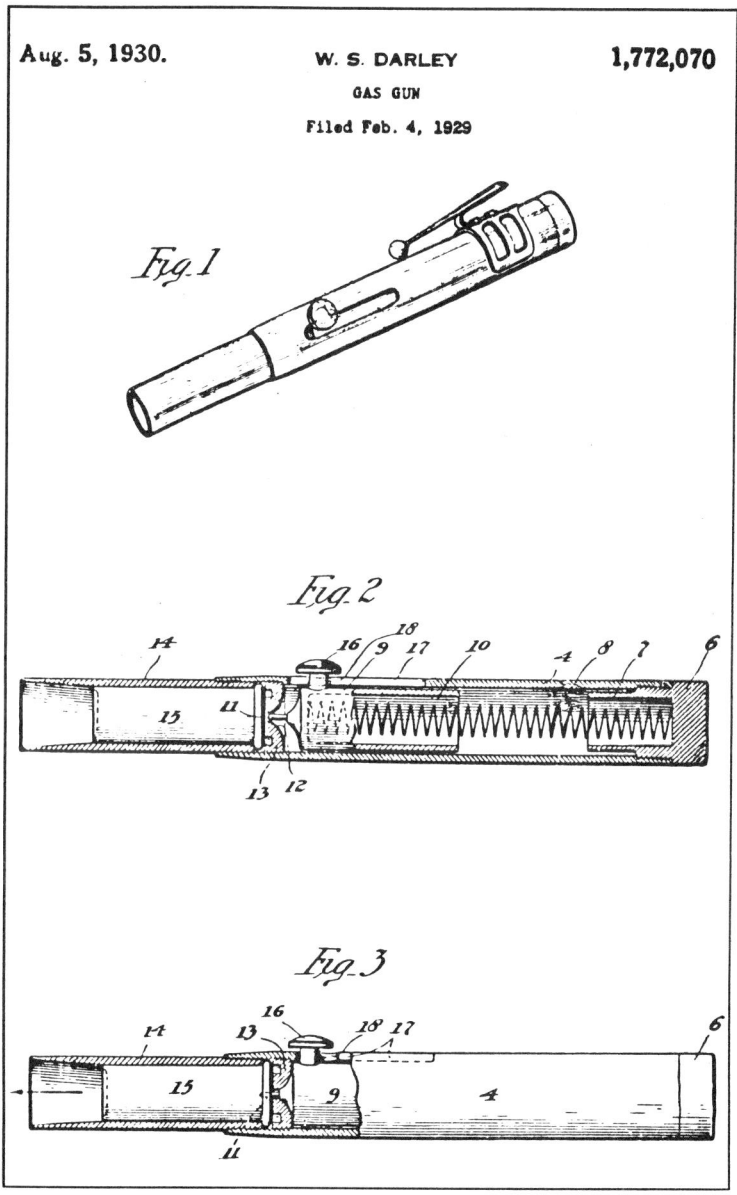

The gas pen gun shown here in W.S. Darley's patent is a simple mechanism featuring a novel breech. (Author redrawing of Darley patent)

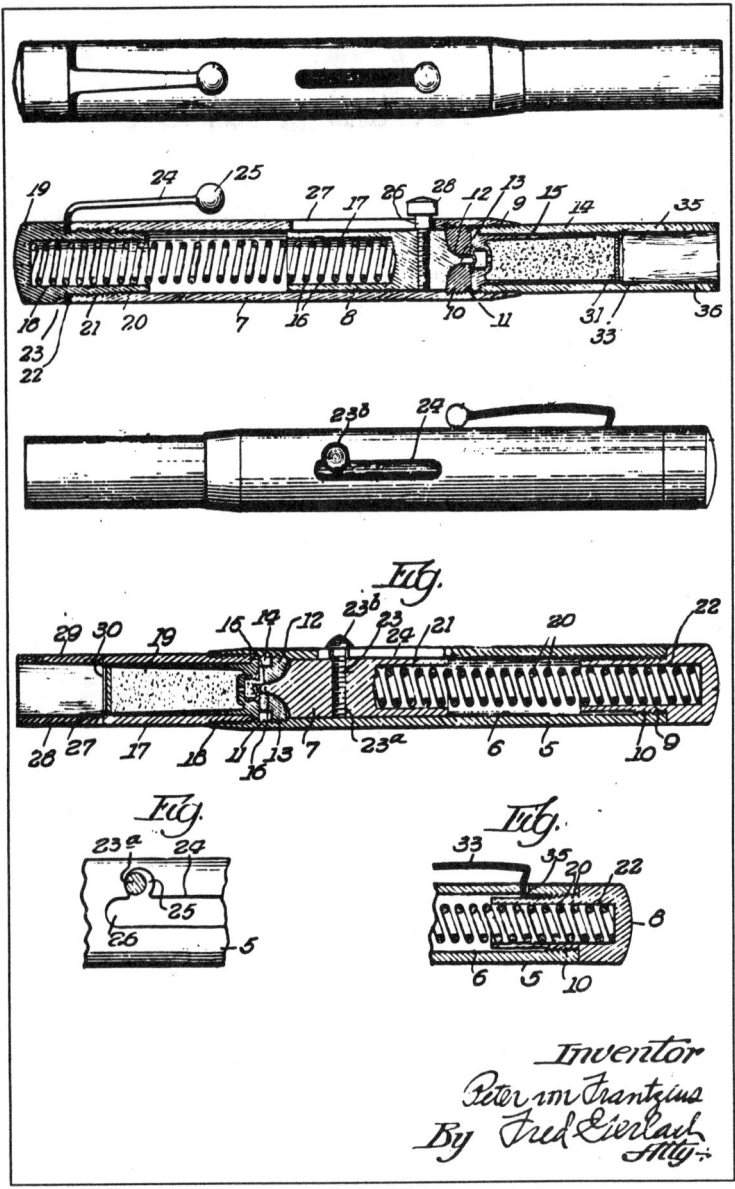

Pen guns developed by Peter Von Frantzius with and without a safety slot. They feature novel pocket clip attachments. (Author redrawing of Von Frantzius patent)

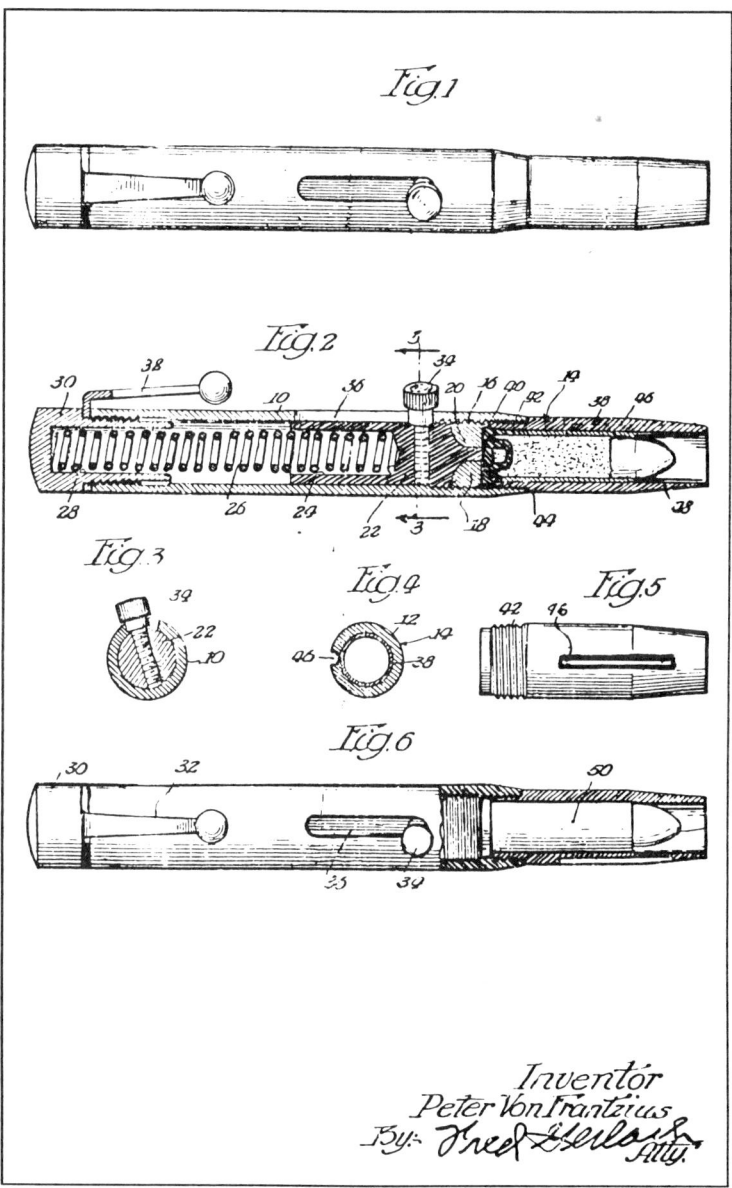

Von Frantzius pen gun with spanner slot for unscrewing barrel for reloading. It has a simple pull-release firing mechanism. (Author redrawing of Von Frantzius patent)

52 / Fingertip Firepower: Pen Guns, Knives, and Bombs

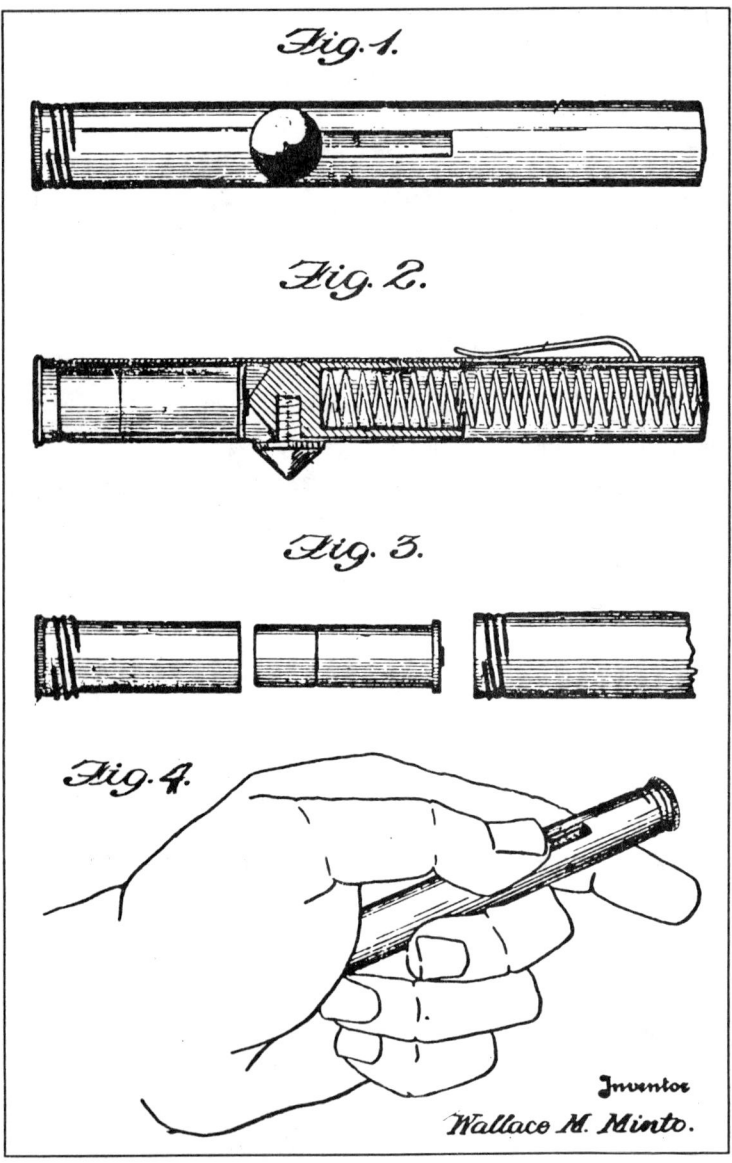

The Minto pen gun. Based on a lipstick-tube design, it has an extruded casing and barrel with raised threads. It is a simple, easily mass-produced pistol. (Author redrawing of Minto patent)

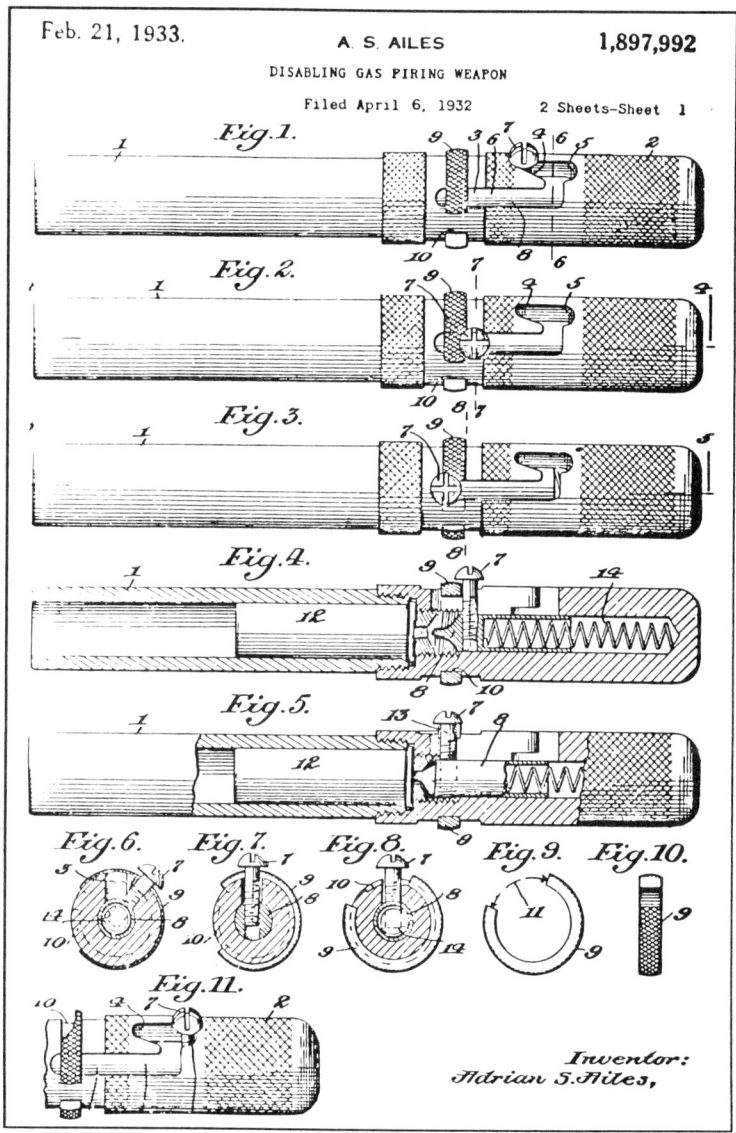

The ring safety device shown in A.S. Ailes' patent (shown here and on following page) has been incorporated into many subsequent pen gun models, including the MAC Stinger. The safety cocking slot was another innovation. (Author redrawing of Ailes patent)

54 / Fingertip Firepower: Pen Guns, Knives, and Bombs

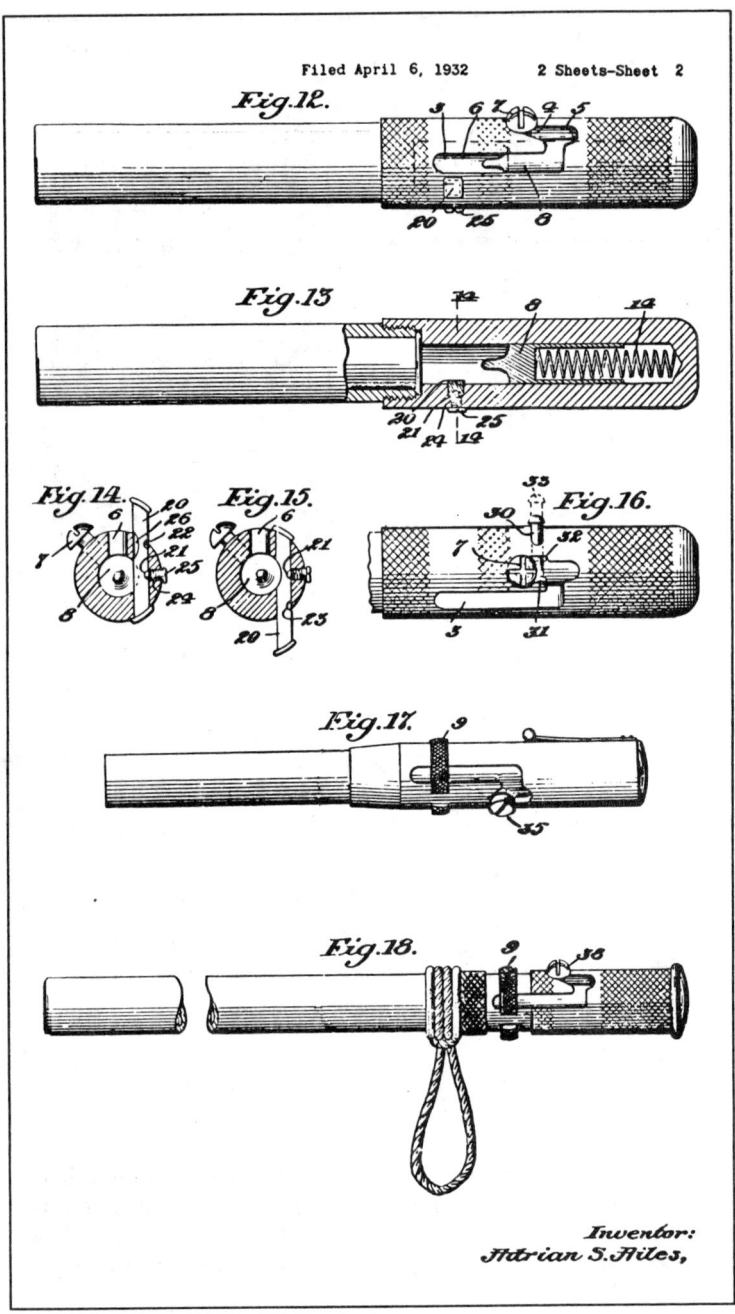

Centerfire Pen Guns

The pen guns in this category evolved out of the tear gas designs of the 1920s. There were some novelty pens used during that decade that fired .32-caliber blanks, and S-2 (U.S. Army Intelligence) had developed centerfire pen devices, mainly for incendiary sabotage or poisoning. But gas was the terror weapon of World War I—many soldiers who survived gassing suffered its brutal aftereffects for years following the Great War. Tear gas, developed by the French, was an asphyxiating agent that precipitated the use of poison gas in warfare.

Law-enforcement officials realized that tear gas could be used for quelling prison disturbances and dispersing violent strikers. Gas guns, truncheons, and pen guns were developed to dispense powdered tear gas and found a ready market in the troubled post-war and Depression years. The very threat to use gas was often enough to subdue violent criminals. It was not treated with the disdain that it is nowadays, as demonstrators come specially equipped to deal with gas munitions.

The first gas pen gun was developed by Dr. Byron C. Goss in 1926 and could fire either gas cartridges or bullets. Many other designs followed, but the most significant were those of Scott M. Abbot, Peter Von Frantzius (who had the Thompson submachine gun franchise in Chicago during the Roaring Twenties), and Adrian S. Ailes. These men patented pen guns that incorporated features found in nearly every subsequent weapon. These units, if they weren't already able to do so, could easily be adapted to fire regular centerfire ammunition. The most popular caliber was .38 Special. (Test firings of unmodified pen guns with constricted chambers have shown that it *is* possible to fire the gun, though it isn't advisable to do so. Upon firing, the bullet squeezes through the undersize bore, leaving a lead ring behind.)

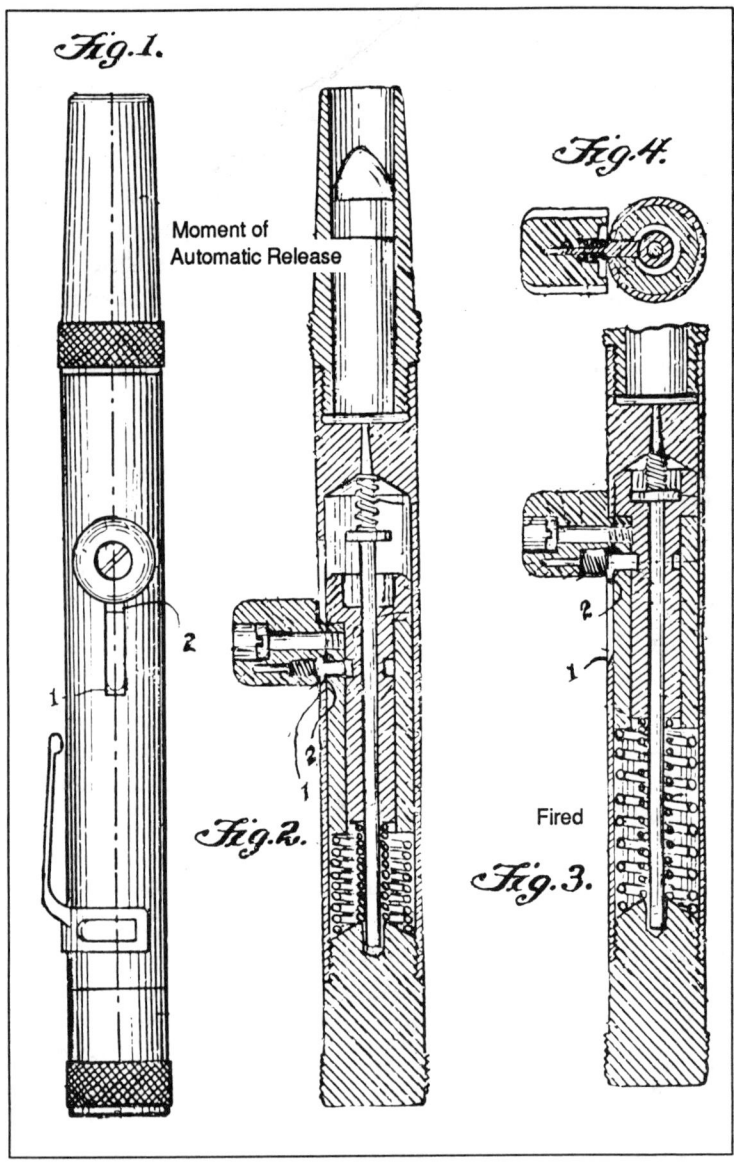

Patent of the Safety pen gun by Don C. Williams. The firing pin is kept away from the primer. When drawn backwards, the cocking knob releases the striker bolt. (Author redrawing of Williams patent)

Shotshell Pen Guns

Like the previous group, the shotshell pen gun grew out of tear-gas devices, which typically had adapters that allowed the firing of gas cartridges of .405 (.44-40), .410, and .20 gauge. In no way should a pen gun be loaded with regular shotgun ammo of those gauges unless the charge has been reduced, the barrel strengthened, and breech reinforced. Case lengths will have to be shortened in some instances to allow for insertion into many pen guns.

In these dimensions the pen gun is harder to conceal, so its appeal is more in handiness than camouflage. It is also the only size that I can recommend for use as a tear-gas gun. The smaller calibers up to .38 Special just don't carry enough agent to do the job of asphyxiating to the point of incapacitation.

There are several modifications that will allow for the use of "snake load" pistol ammo, which contains birdshot (a .22 snake-load cartridge is available commercially). Expended pen gun flare cartridges can be reloaded with such BB-shot loads.

The advantages of firing shot are twofold: it is an excellent Stinger load for dissuasion and, as pen guns are so inaccurate, it increases the chances of a hit. The BB-shot flaregun load, for example, is capable of inflicting lethal injuries, and even .22 lead dust loads can blind an adversary. At extremely close ranges, there is no real difference in stopping power since the densely packed charge is like a solid projectile. Out to ten feet, however, a bullet is still the best choice for serious injuries.

Rockets and Flares

Advances in miniature rocketry over the past thirty years have made it possible to construct pen rocket launchers. Pen flareguns have rocket elements and therefore can be grouped in this category as well.

58 / Fingertip Firepower: Pen Guns, Knives, and Bombs

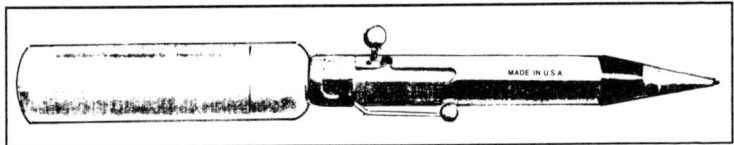

The Hagen .410 tear-gas pencil gun. The unusual design incorporates the firing mechanism into the end of a mechanical pencil. (Author drawing)

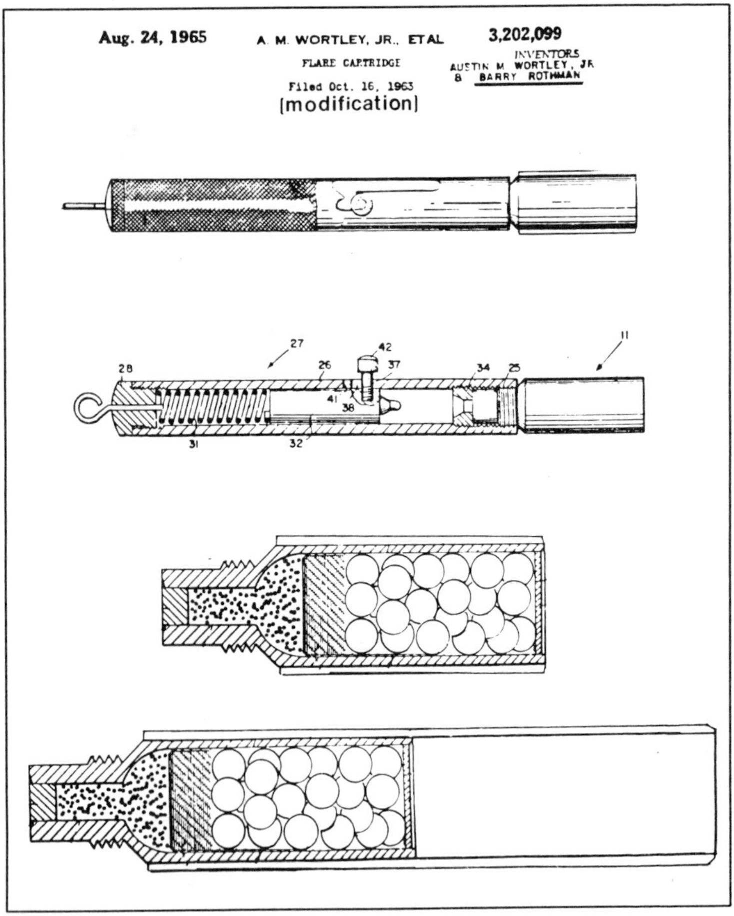

The Wortley/Rothman patent showing a flare cartridge converted to fire twenty-eight BBs. Note the reinforcement to the cartridge case. (Author redrawing of Wortley/Rothman patent)

The miniature rocket was an outgrowth of the space industry, which required small rockets for testing the feasibility of larger designs at reduced expense. Robert Mainhardt of MBA headed a team that designed and built such devices. It quickly dawned on them that the miniature rockets would also make viable weapon projectiles. They went on to build the Gyrojet pistols and carbines, which enjoyed modest notoriety, if not success, in the 1960s. It was an idea ahead of its time.

The Gyrojet was criticized in gun circles for the fact that at close ranges the velocity of its rocket was not substantial enough to cause injury, and there were statements that it would bounce off cardboard at five feet. Since rockets build thrust during flight, these were valid points. What wasn't considered was that the rocket could be held back momentarily, allowing it to build thrust, by increasing the tension on the hammer spring holding it back (like the chocks at Cape Kennedy). The hesitation required would be slightly less than instantaneous with these minirockets.

The powerful minirockets had great appeal since they were recoilless and could be launched "from soda straws," as Mr. Mainhardt claimed during his sales pitches. They didn't even require barrels since they were stabilized by gyroscopic venting of the rocket's exhaust gases. The rockets were fueled with a version of regular double-based pistol powder and were fired by percussion primer. MBA designed underwater versions, machine guns, and launch tubes in cigarette and pen configurations. Clandestine agency interest was high.

The use of flares fired from pen-like devices goes back to the transition from sail to steam, before radio was developed. The perils of ship navigation required the stocking of flares and rockets to signal distress. The American Coston Flare was a pocket-sized signal device. True pen flareguns were designed for the survival kits of downed aircrews of the Strategic Air

Three examples of pen-gun conversions. The weapon at right is a commercial blank gun made in Italy. It will not chamber bulleted cartridges but can be bored out to take .22 BB or CB caps. The middle device is the same unit with another pocket clip endcap screwed into the muzzle. It can be easily bored to accommodate .22 Shorts or Longs. The flaregun at left demonstrates the same facility. Mob loan sharks have been known to use such weapons to "sting" the legs of recalcitrant borrowers. (Author photo)

Comparison of two flareguns (right). The gun at right, made by Life Support Technology, uses a large cast-aluminum thumb-slip striker release. The mechanism slot is never exposed. The device at left is Penguin Industries' commercial version. Both units have a 300-foot range. (Author photo)

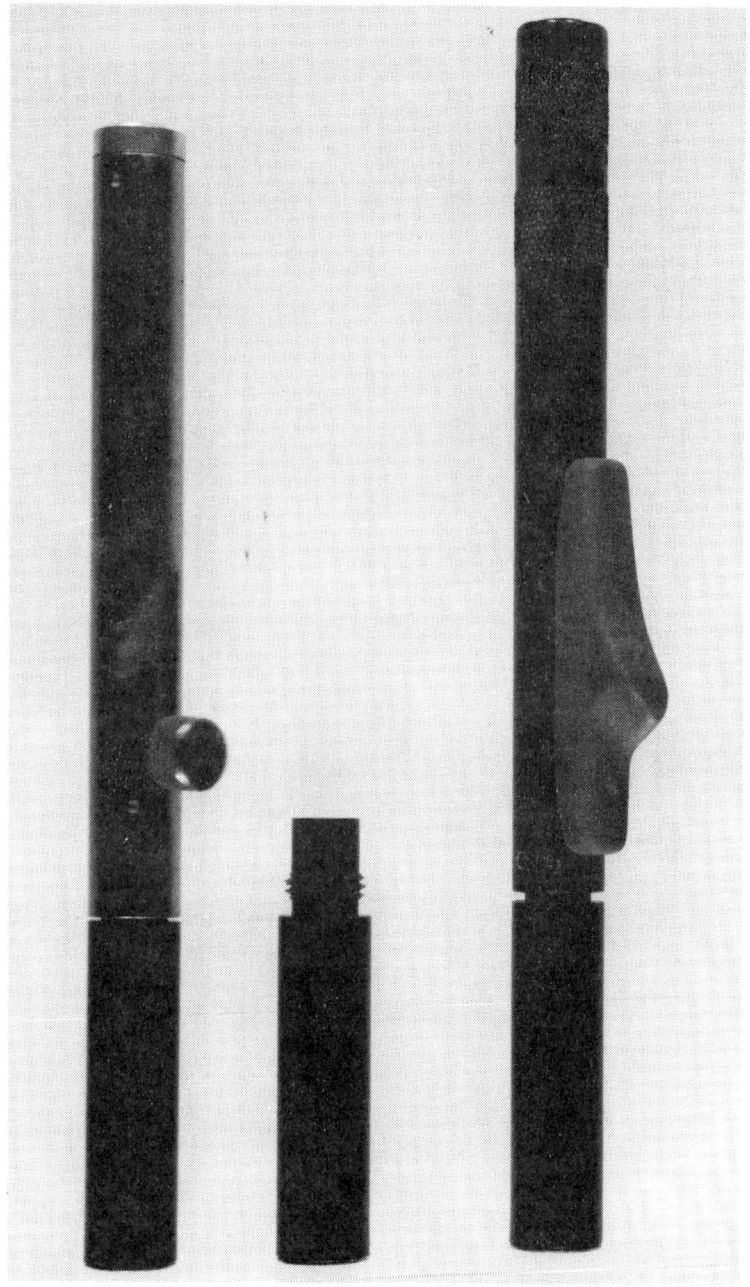

62 / *Fingertip Firepower: Pen Guns, Knives, and Bombs*

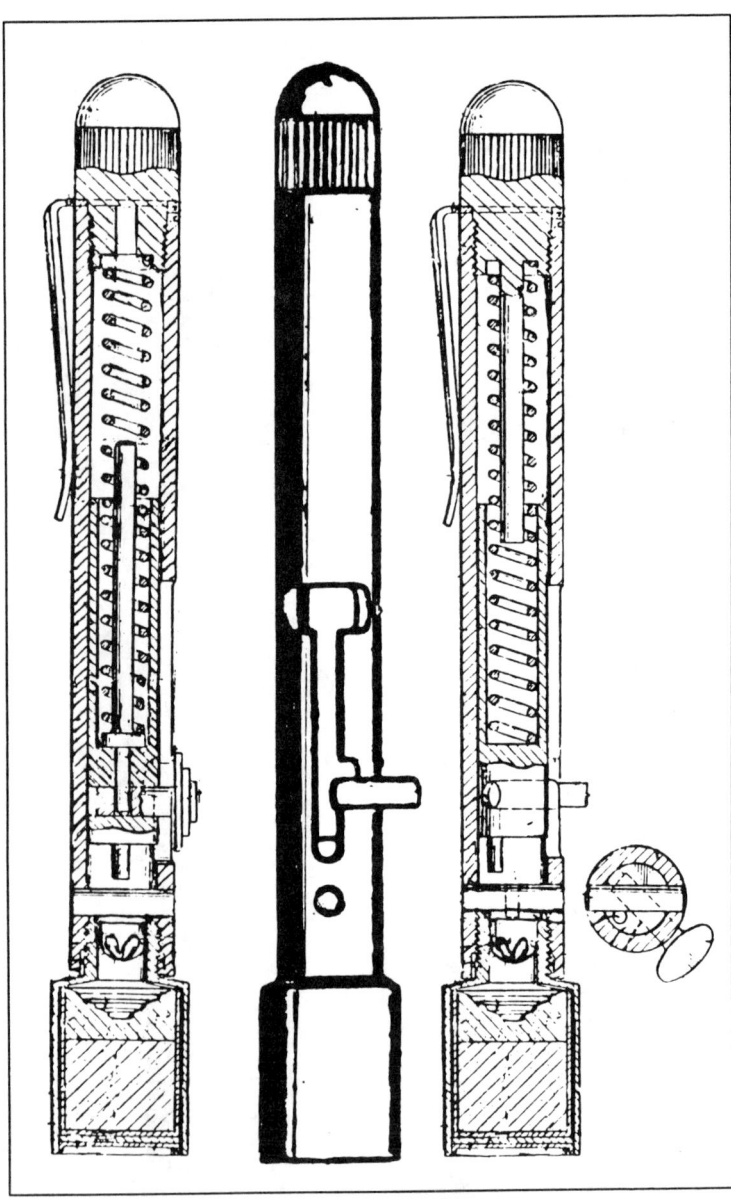

Two versions of a rocket flaregun that uses a .22 blank to ignite the flare. This device can easily be converted to fire regular .22 ammo. (Author redrawing of Stefan patent)

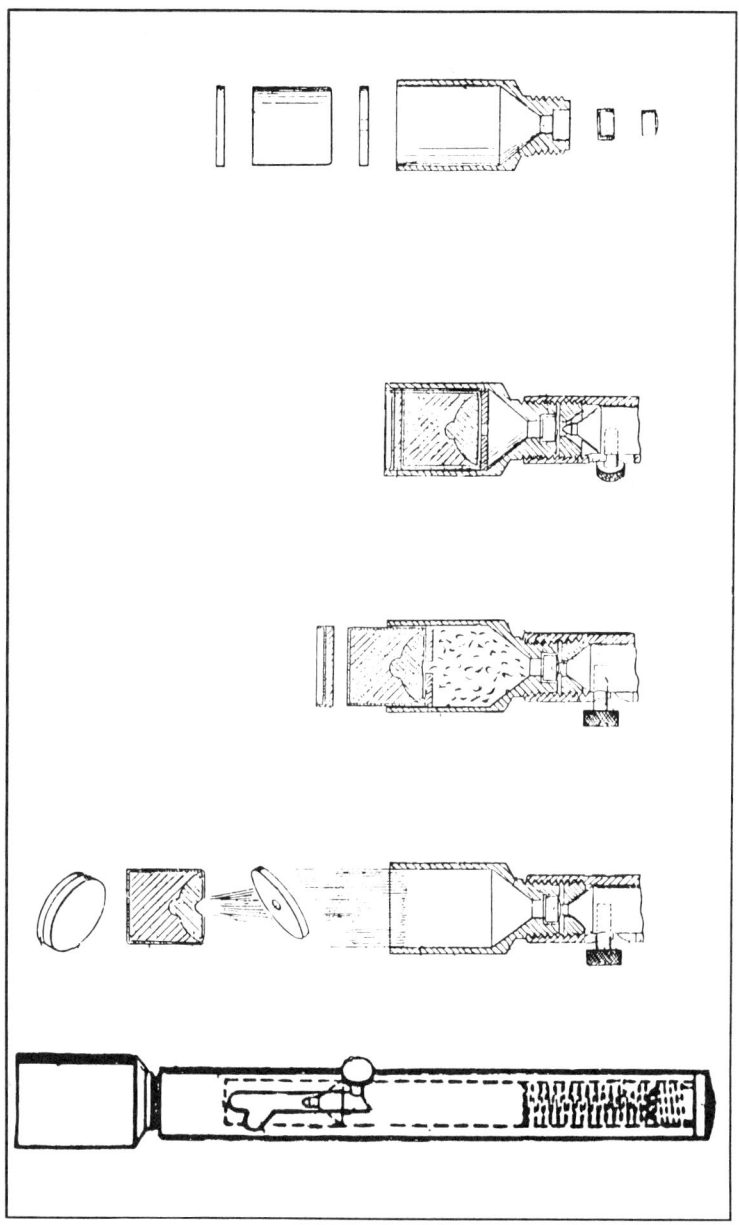

Third version of the Stefan rocket flaregun showing construction details and launch sequence. (Author redrawing of Stefan patent)

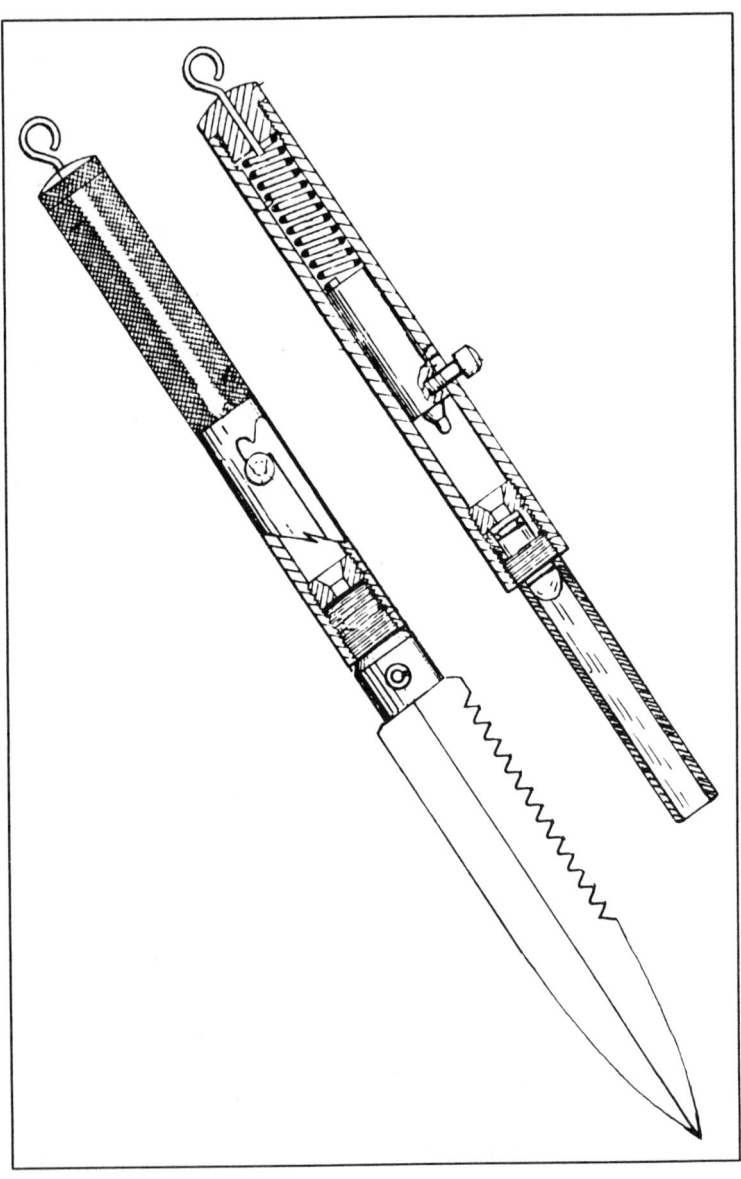

Modifications of the military survival flaregun. The screw-in dagger is based on the CIA frisk knife. The .25 ACP (6.35mm) barrel adapter allows the unit to be fired as a pen gun as well. (Author drawing)

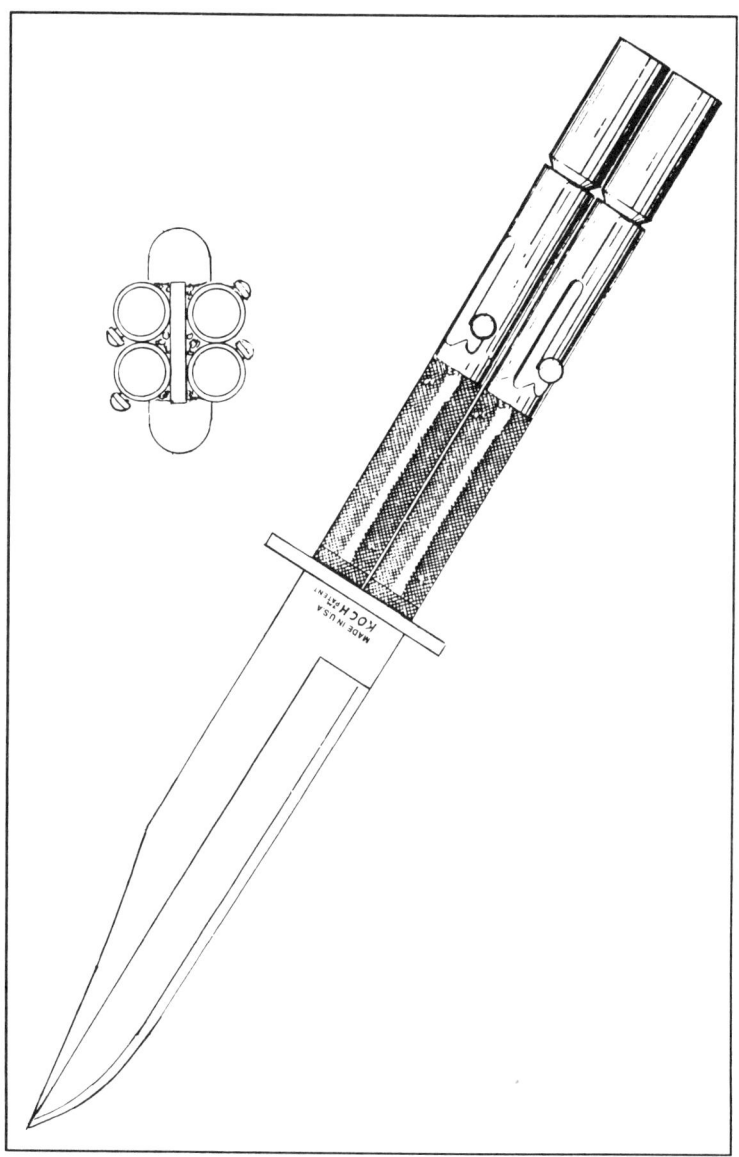

Bob Koch of Research, California, contributed this idea for a four-shot survival knife. Either flares or conversion cartridges may be used. Pen bodies are epoxied to knife tang to form a solid grip handle. (Author drawing)

Command. They were quickly copied by companies that catered to civilian pilots, boaters, and outdoorsmen.

The most popular design was probably that of Penguin Industries Inc., which grew out of research by Barry Rothman, who also designed tear gas pen guns, the poisoned felt-tip marker, and the exploding .22 round. (Rothman was the subject of a *Playboy* article entitled "Mr. Death" and a book of the same title written by his son.) An earlier patent by Russell Stefan is also worthy of note; it uses a .22 blank to launch a rocket-assisted flare approximately one hundred yards into the air. A survival flare gun made by SAC, Inc. is the only unit that can fire MBA rockets without having to be modified to do so.

The alteration of these items into bullet and shot weapons has already been established. They can also be used as weapons in their own right. Taxi drivers in Toronto, Canada, were arming themselves with pen flareguns after a series of robberies where cabbies were being knifed to death. The effects of firing an incendiary-like flare into the rear seat of a taxi would startle any attacker long enough for the driver to flee. The flare could be shot into an assailant's face, neck, or clothing as well. A long thumbtack or straightened fishing hook could be epoxied to the flare to prevent it from bouncing off an assailant. Firm contact could even bury a burning flare under the skin.

Macro and Multishot Pen Guns

Larger-sized pen guns were part of an evolutionary process toward a more powerful tubular weapon that could pass notice as a shipper's marker pen or novelty pocket item. The four-inch-long .32-caliber Webber squeezer pistol was patented in 1905 and was certainly small enough to be concealed as a pen gun. However it inspired later designs that were much larger, such as the squeezer firearms invented by Merle Gill in 1933 and the wondrous "Krupp Karl Kash Super Weapon," designed in 1975.

All of these weapons fire in the same manner. The index and middle fingers pull a ring or sliding member rearward along the barrel, cocking the firing pin until it disengages and the weapon fires. The butt rests against the fleshy part of the hand at the base of the thumb.

I am indebted to Rick Hummell, staff writer of the *Kerrville Daily Times*, Kerrville, Texas, who interviewed Karl Kash in July 1982 and who described the inventor's weapon: "The single-shot pistol is about four-inches long, one-inch wide and looks like a stubby blue hypodermic needle." He goes on to quote from the brochure: "The Super Weapon is the fastest, most powerful .357 primary backup for a survival weapon in the world. Ideal for law enforcement, bodyguards, survival, home defense, any type of dangerous, clandestine or covert missions. It can be fired underwater, any depth, in mud and sand; can penetrate a one-eighth-inch steel plate making a 2-inch hole; can penetrate 50 plies of bulletproof cloth; and is 100 percent concealable in a special hand glove or belt holster."

Kash had to invent the gun because standard pistols could not accommodate his ammunition, which he claimed was "ten times more powerful than factory-produced .357 ammunition." Kash's other claim that he had created "a new form of physics: ultra-super hyper force" aside, he had indeed created a powerful pen gun on the basis that it fires .357 Magnum ammo. Yet it looked so much like a pen gun to the Bureau of Alcohol, Tobacco and Firearms that it was classified as "any other weapon."

The Kash gun came equipped with syringe-like finger grips. The inventor later tried to make it more acceptable to the BATF by affixing a small standard pistol grip. A blank-firing version was also made (the

68 / Fingertip Firepower: Pen Guns, Knives, and Bombs

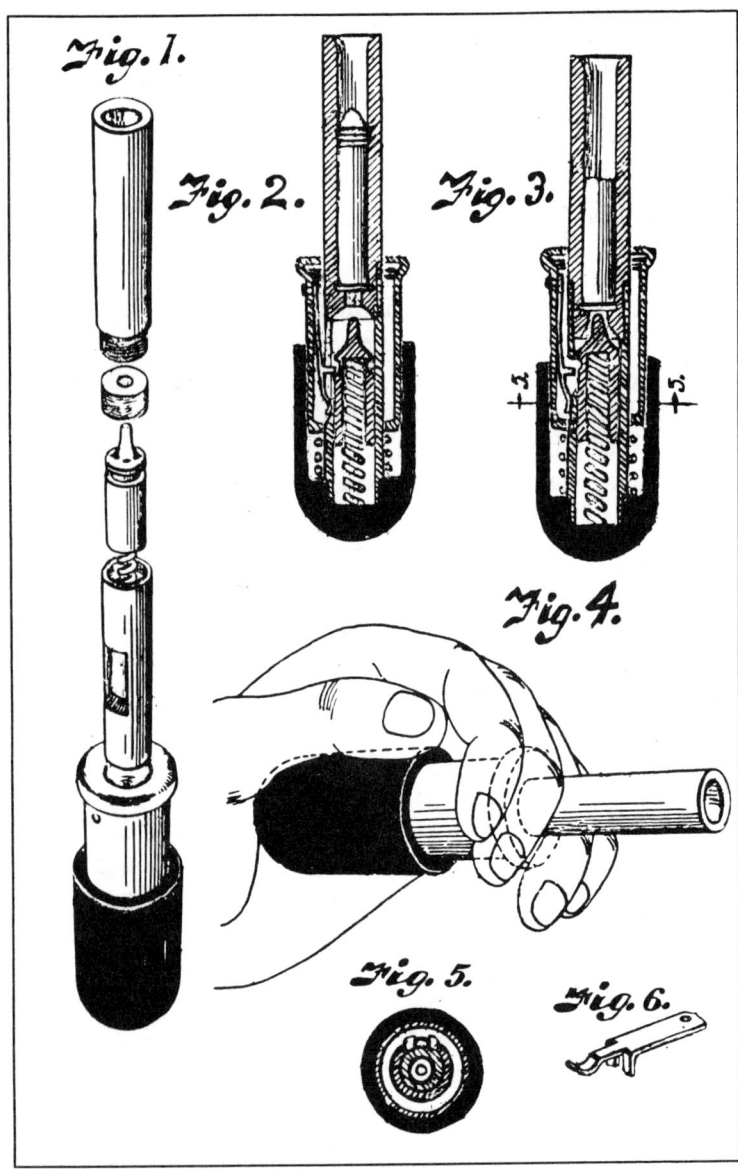

This squeezer pistol straddles the Webber design and the Kash gun. As the firing pin is forced back, a projection on the retractor spring rides up a slope, ultimately releasing the firing pin. (Author redrawing of Gill patent)

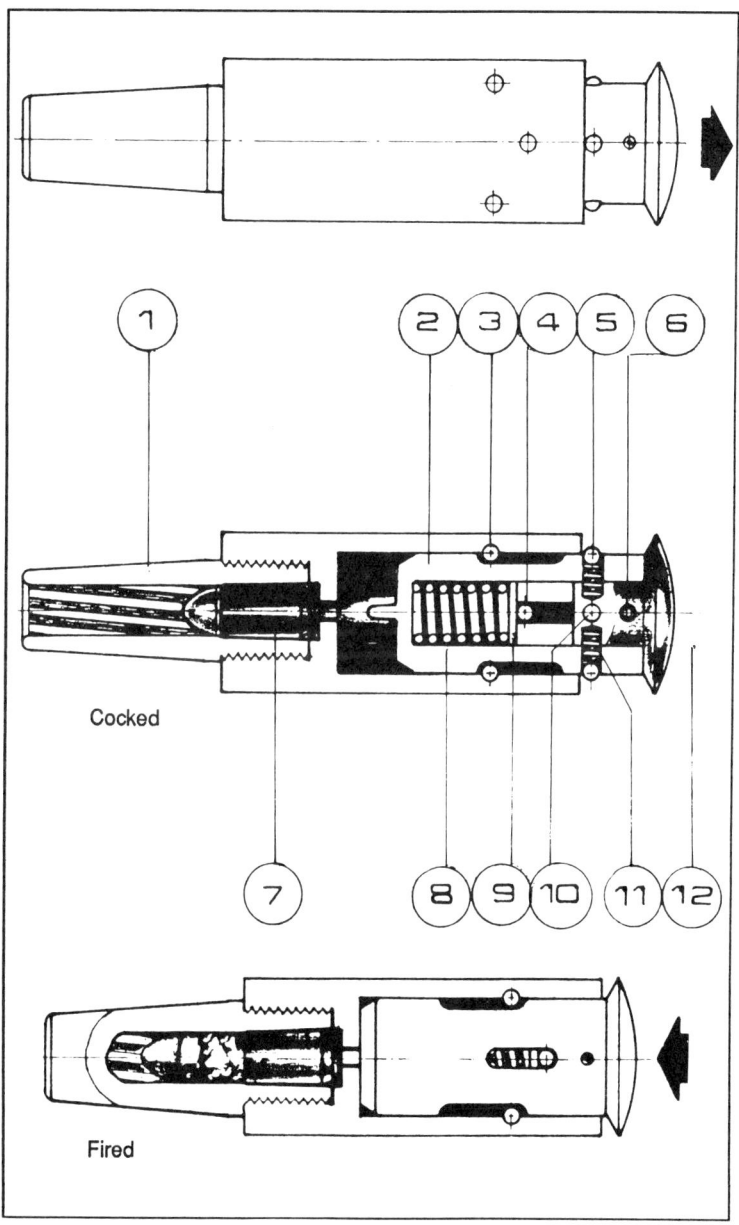

A simplified version of the Kash pistol (Illustration courtesy of Joe Ramos)

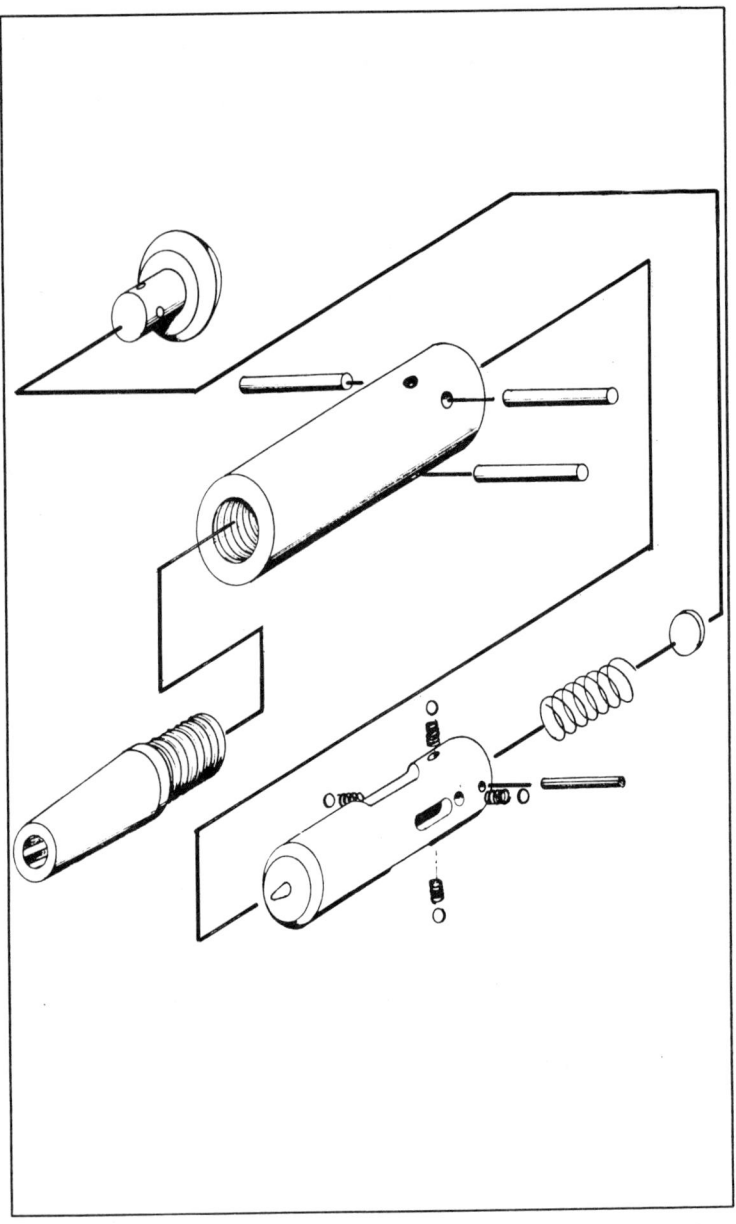

Parts breakdown of the simplified Kash pistol. (Illustration courtesy of Joe Ramos)

Karl Kash firing his super pistol. (Photo courtesy of Rick Hummell, *Kerrville Daily Times*, Kerrville, Texas)

cartridges were not interchangeable). In light of Kash's claim about an "ultra-super hyper force," I can only make the observation that it may simply be concentrated muzzle blast—a reverse silencer, if you will.

The most obvious multishot version of the pen gun is the double-ender, where the weapon can be turned around to fire a quick second shot without extracting the first empty shell. The barrel is threaded at both ends. Typically, these pen guns have two L-slot portions and firing pin bolts, but both ends share a common mainspring. They cannot be cocked simultaneously, so murder/suicide is not an option. Nevertheless, one should always be conscious of which end is cocked and where the muzzle is pointing. There is a 20-gauge macro version called the Hagen Dictator Tear Gas Club that can be modified to fire downloaded ammunition.

Holders for placing two pen guns side-by-side have been developed, as have several makes of twin-barrelled guns. The L-slot pen gun release is probably best

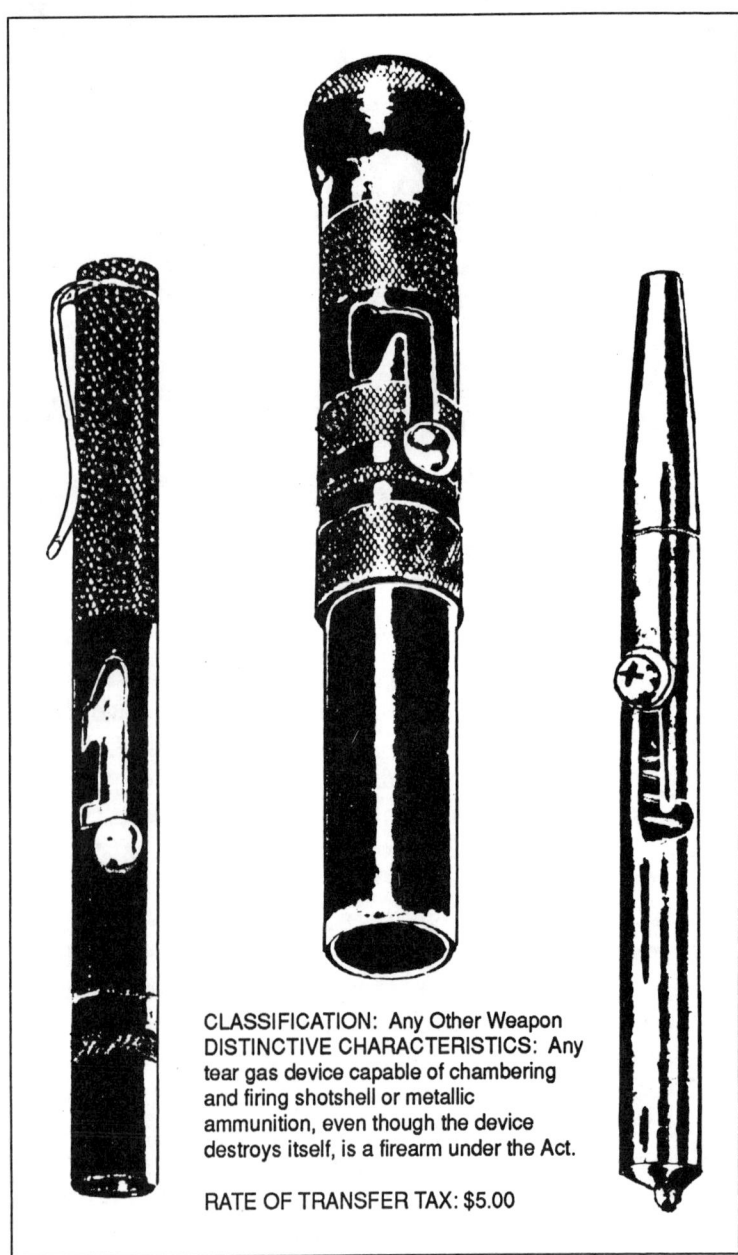

BATF classification of pen guns. (Illustration courtesy of BATF)

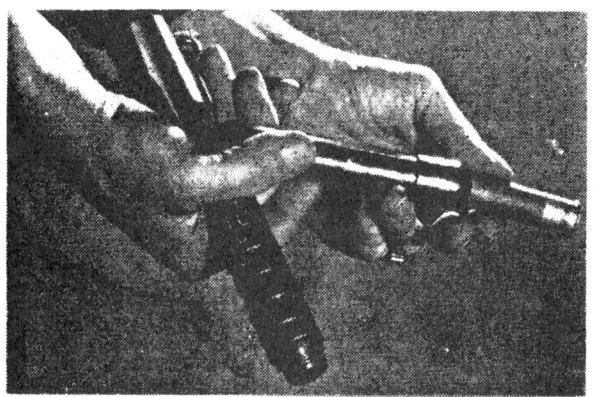

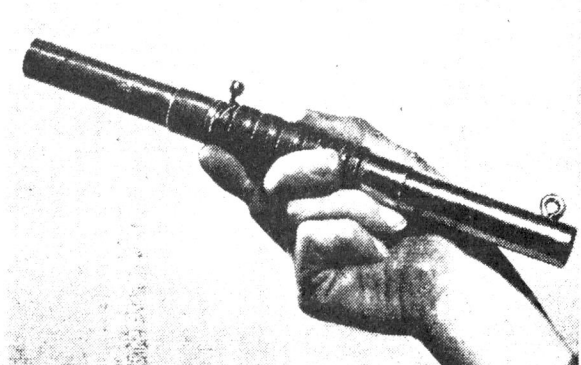

The Hagen Dictator double-ender 20-gauge gas gun. Several makers of .22 gas guns also made double enders. (Photo courtesy of the Chicago Police Department)

exemplified in the West German Gatling gun replica, which mounts ten bolts radially and releases the firing levers by rotating them against a fixed stop. It does not automatically load or eject like the original Gatling. The ammunition must be preloaded and the breeches tightened to the barrels, then each bolt is cocked within its respective L-slot. Advancing the barrels and bolts through a worm-gear drive completes the Gatling illusion. The device is often used for contemporary reenactments of historical battles.

A miniature machine gun could be made from pen

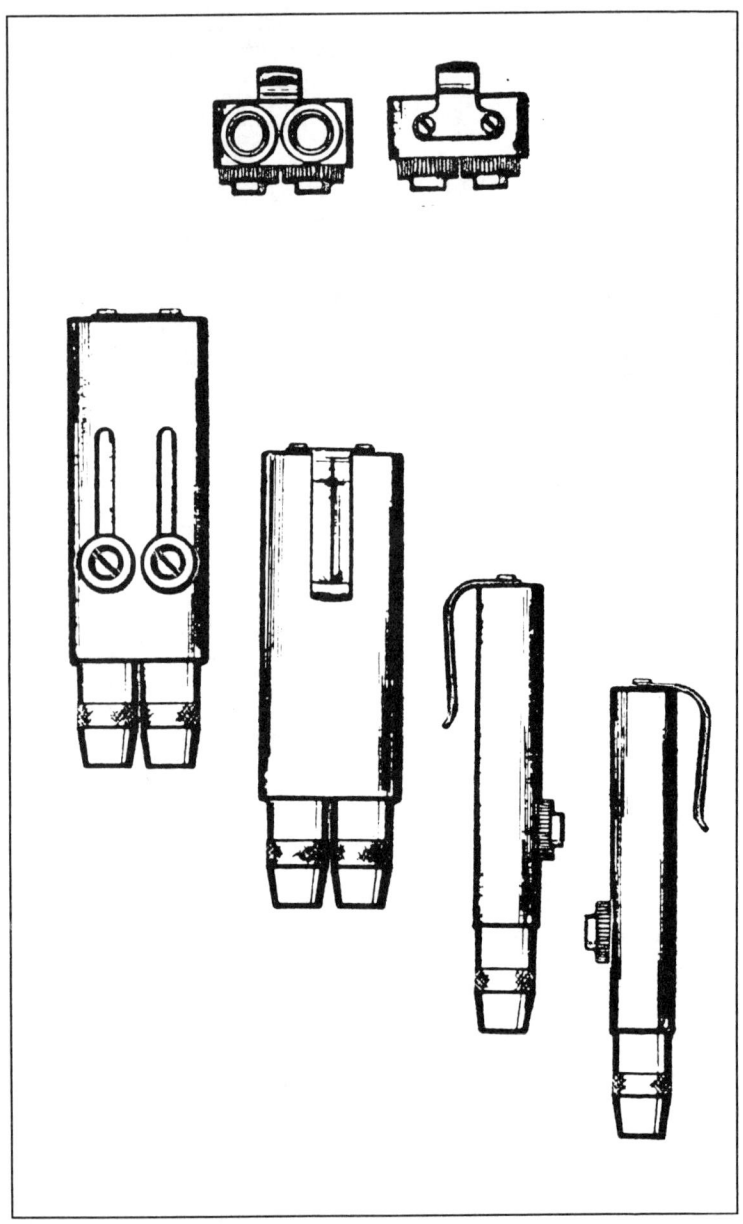

Hiser double-barreled tear gas gun. (Author redrawing of Hiser patent)

guns as a personal weapon, but a scrap cylinder from a .22-revolver mounted on an eccentric axis attached to a pen gun would serve the same purpose. Some commercial miniature flareguns have a similar capability.

Pen Gun Safety Procedures

Pen guns are extremely prone to accidental discharge. The main culprit for this condition is the bolt's firing pin. It rests against the base of the cartridge when fully forward and ostensibly safe. In the classic L-slot pen gun there is a cocking slot that allows the bolt to be retracted rearward, and in some pen guns there is a side slot that allows the bolt to remain in the cocked position until the weapon is ready to be fired. (Some models also have a safety slot cut out near the breech, which allows the bolt firing pin to be parked clear of the cartridge primer.)

The very portability of the pen gun works against its safety. It is commonly carried in the breast pocket, where it is clipped to the garment like other pens. What is not often appreciated is that pen guns are considerably heavier than regular pens and so, when the owner bends over to tie a shoelace or pick up dropped change, the weapon might slip out and fall base forwards against the floor. This impact is often enough to disengage the cocked bolt and fire the gun or, conversely but just as perversely, cause a safetied bolt to bounce rearward (like the Sten submachine guns of yore) and then fire. (An actual incident occurred just along those lines. The pen gun hit the ground, discharged, and shot the owner's wife under the chin, killing her.)

When letting down a cocked bolt, the little knob can slip out of one's grip and cause an accidental discharge. This happened to me on one occasion. Fortunately a blank cartridge was involved, but the experience was salutary: I now first unscrew the barrel before letting down the bolt.

The little cocking knob can also break away, unscrew, or rotate out of position by the combined action of abrasion against clothes and body movement. The owner must be aware of any activity that might impinge on the safe carry or operation of his weapon.

Pen gun ammunition must, in most cases, be reloaded downward (in *all* cases with larger calibers). Firing regular ammo in a pen gun is an invitation to disaster. The guns are too small and light to handle the recoil, and it is even difficult to hold one in the fingertips during discharge. American and British intelligence and espionage agencies recognized this limitation and thus trained their operatives to allow .22 Stinger guns to recoil out of the hand while directed away from the body.

Another actual incident accentuates this point. I was once shown a series of gruesome photos and X-rays where an individual had aimed and fired a .45 ACP pen gun. The results were horrific. The weapon fired without damage, but the pen recoiled out of the shooter's hands along the line-of-sight and entered his right eye, burying itself in his brain. 'Nough said.

A wartime case illustrates just how confusing pen guns can be even to the initiated. An OSS instructor in China was demonstrating how to use the Stinger to a classroom of agents. He held it backwards in his hand and shot himself in the stomach. In yet another incident, the Military Armaments Corporation SSSW Stinger was being demonstrated to potential buyers when the salesman, who was familiar with the weapon to the point of nonchalance, placed his opposite hand in front of the muzzle while he fired. The round guttered across several fingers.

Always treat these little weapons with a great deal of respect; they are man killers and often can bite the hand that feeds them.

CHAPTER FIVE
PEN BOMBS AND MINES

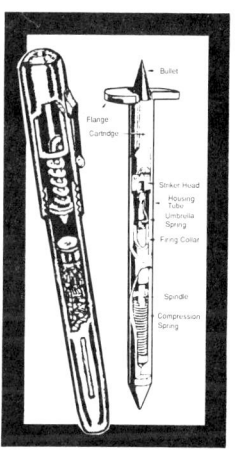

Pen guns are disguised, concealable, and handy personal weapons. The pen bomb has similar attributes. It is used chiefly as a booby-trap device in locations where pens are likely to be encountered publicly, such as banks, post offices, and government agencies. Pens left lying around are invariably scooped up, and eventually a person will unscrew it to examine the condition of the nib. A sharp crack and explosion—flame, smoke, and shrapnel will engulf the upper body. Another victim maimed, blinded, possibly killed.

The pen bomb is a device that can trap all but the most wary. It is seemingly harmless and is therefore an unlikely candidate for a terror weapon, which makes it an effective choice for a terror weapon. The most recent use of pen bombs was in the war in Afghanistan, where the Soviets were accused of dropping them into villages along with booby-trapped toys designed to appeal to children. Pen bombs show up in every war, however, and are used by both sides; it only depends on whose ox

78 / *Fingertip Firepower: Pen Guns, Knives, and Bombs*

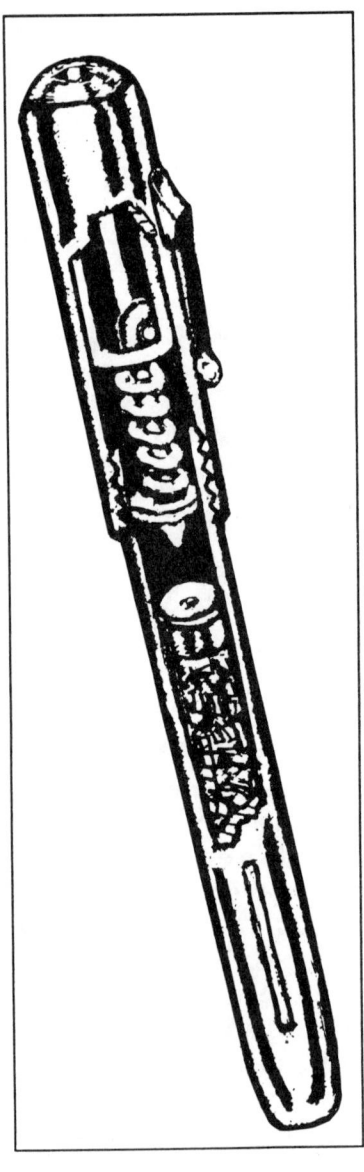

British pen bomb booby trap. (Author redrawing based on illustration from British Army Royal Engineers pamphlet)

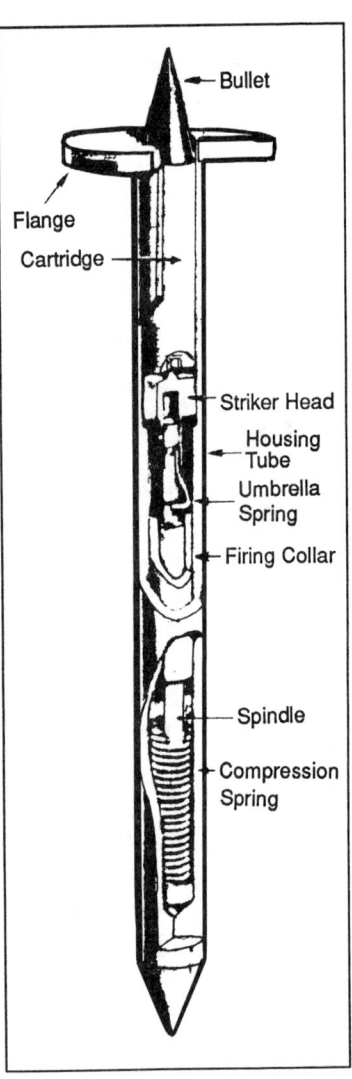

A cutaway drawing of an M.D. 1 AP Switch, or ground spike pistol, showing location of parts. (Author redrawing based on illustration from British Army Royal Engineers pamphlet)

is being gored when blame is being placed. The British, who used them first, targeted Gestapo officers and other members of the Nazi infrastructure. The Japanese used them against American GIs, who were notorious souvenir hounds. They have since shown up in conflicts worldwide, from Indochina to Algeria.

The British design illustrated on the facing page is precocked. The L-shaped firing pin is held back by an L-shaped hook. The short bases of the L interconnect but will rotate free from each other when the cap and body are unscrewed. When released, the firing pin strikes a percussion primer and detonates the charge. Low-order explosives and photoflash mixtures can be used to cause shock and burn trauma. The design can easily be altered to fire a bullet. (The prison-made match-head pen bomb also shares this capability.)

The M.D. 1 (Ministry of Defence 1) AP (antipersonnel) Switch—also known as a ground spike pistol but more commonly, if not accurately, known as the "Castrator" mine—was originally developed by the British in World War I (U.S. manuals incorrectly attribute it to the Germans) for roadblocking and airfield defense. It fired a steel bullet upward to pierce tires that rolled over the weapon's tip.

The unit was essentially a drawn steel tube that could be hammered into the ground like a tent peg. A cocked firing mechanism was slipped into the tube, topped off with a round now known to collectors as the ".40 Booby." The mechanism was restrained by an umbrella-like spring catch over which slid a firing-pin tube. When the bullet was depressed by a tire or a foot, it pushed down on the firing-pin tube, forcing the umbrella catch inward and allowing the cocked firing collar to ride up a spindle, striking a smart blow on the firing pin and discharging the round. If trod upon, the round could bore through the foot and impact into the groin, hence the "castrator" appellation. It could also

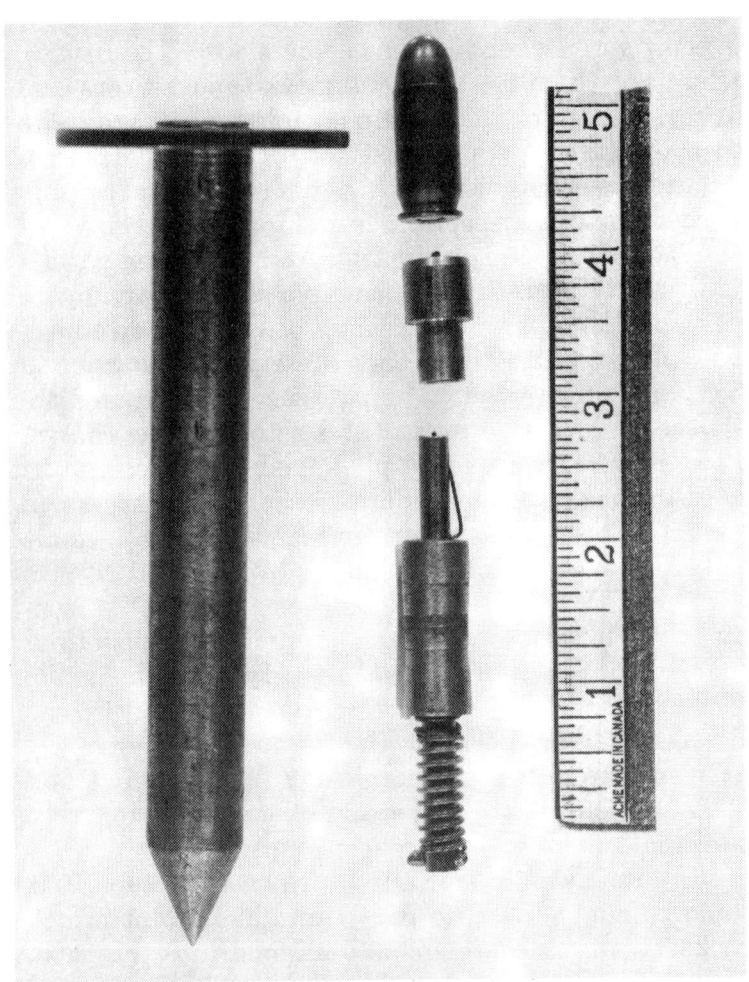

Homemade .45 ACP version of a ground spike pistol. (Author photo)

bypass that area and strike under the chin.

The M.D. 1 AP Switch is the size of a pen gun and may be used as a pistol by jamming the muzzle into an adversary's body. The device is not difficult to make; the above photo is of a homemade specimen in .45 ACP. Original ground spike pistol ICI rounds are hard to come by but can be made by buffing the rims from .38

Pen Bombs and Mines / 81

Special ammo. A conical steel bullet can be turned to fit and reloaded into the case, but the modified regular round will serve in most instances. The No. 12 High Explosive Switch worked in a similar fashion as the ground spike pistol but was much more devastating, substituting a mini-mine for the bullet.

(Bullet-firing mines are unusual. U.S. Army Special Forces experimented with a plastic mine in Vietnam that fired four 12-gauge shotgun rounds in an upward radial pattern. Used in the same conflict, the VC "toe popper" was made from a bamboo tube and contained a cartridge with thinned primer resting upon a nail.)

Most military time pencils (a pencil-like explosive initiator utilizing a time delay) and pull-fuse igniters also have percussion primer initiators in their firing chain. They therefore can be adapted to fire ammunition within improvised barrels of pen gun proportions, or can be affixed with miniature charges and used as pen bombs.

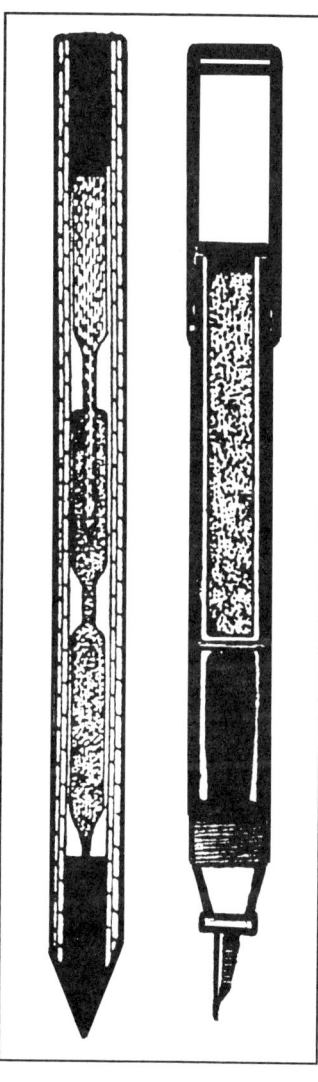

Pen and pencil weapons used in World War I. The unit at right is a toxic fountain pen, at left an incendiary time pencil. (Author redrawing based on illustration from *Spies and the Next War*)

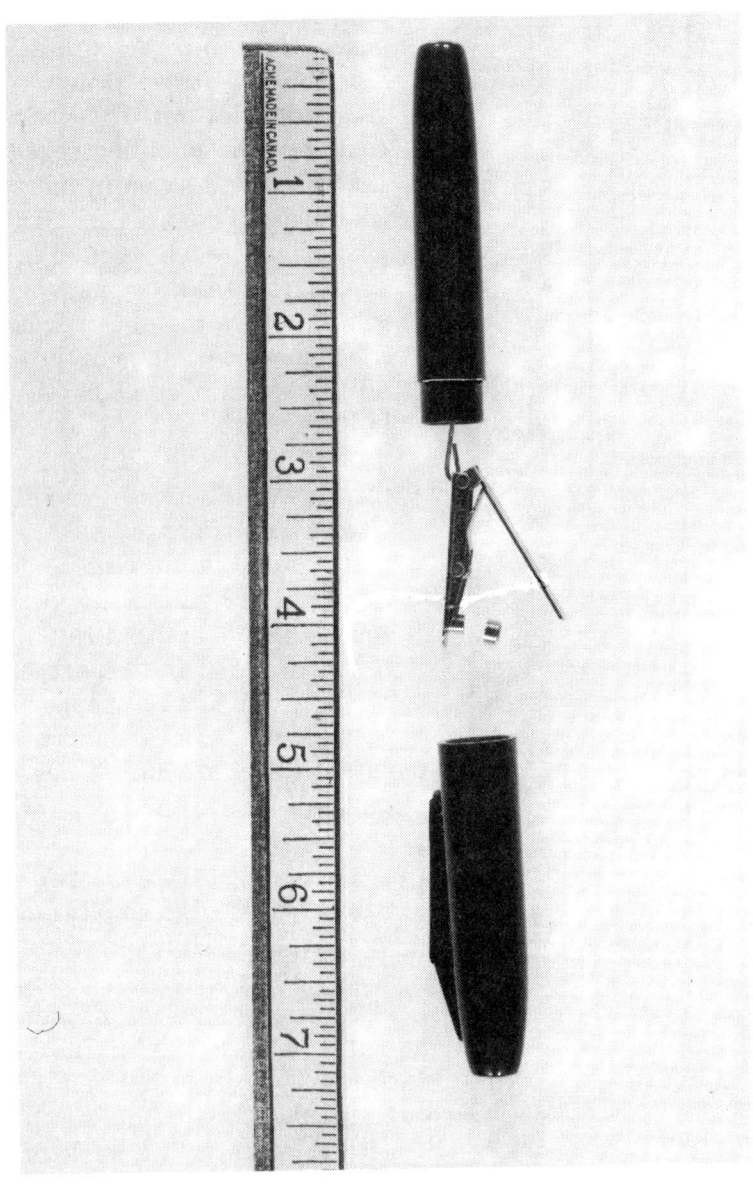

A novelty pen with bouchon igniter and toy cap held down by hinged flap until withdrawn from pen cap. This device gives off a loud report. It can be modified to ignite photoflash powder or explosive. (Author photo)

Time pencils were first used in World War I, when German saboteurs employed incendiary versions in the wharves of French harbors. They were initiated by breaking a sulfuric acid vial, which then acted on a potassium chlorate package, causing the pencil to burst into a searing flame. Similar devices were used in World War II by both sides.

The chemical-delay igniters in time pencils, which ate through the firing-pin spring restraining wires within a set time, were subject to environmental vagaries, so a lead-creep delay igniter was developed. A length of lead was subjected to the stress of being pulled by the firing-pin spring until, at a predetermined time, it would fatigue and fire the device.

In Volume IV of the *How To Kill* series, I included an illustration of a lead-creep-delay pen gun that was to be left on a desk pointing at a seated victim, ready to fire its .32 ACP round once its lead wire gave way at a preset time. An ornamental pen holder that will fire a round at an office visitor when activated is shown on page 84. Ian Skennerton, the Australian firearms writer, told me of a similar desk ornament that projected sharp pins if handled incorrectly, and that the owner had caused many a guest to bleed by encouraging them to handle it. The long, sharp pins were spring-loaded. He suggested that poisoning them could be an option.

Toxic pens were actually issued towards the end of World War I and were only held from employment by the cessation of hostilities. Lucretia Borgia developed a poison ink that would kill the letter's addressee. It might sound farfetched, but a poison powder could be shaken onto a document that would fall into the lap of the recipient when the document was unfolded, killing him.

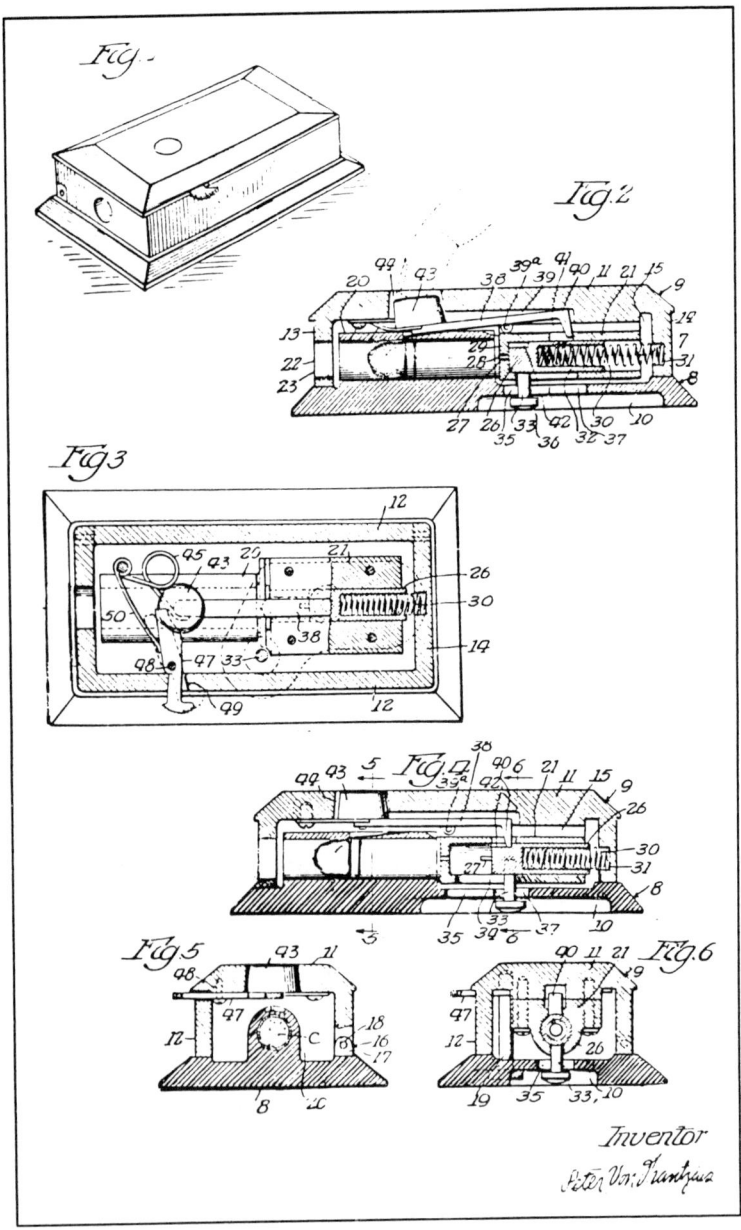

Pistol concealed within a desk ornament. (Author redrawing of Von Frantzius patent)

CHAPTER SIX
SPECIAL SPY WEAPONS

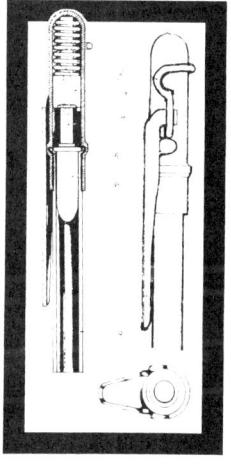

Viet Cong Fountain Pen Assassination Weapon

This weapon is shaped like an ordinary fountain pen with a fastening clip. The pen cap has a groove used for guiding the firing pin. The bolt and firing pin form one piece.

The pen body is made of a smooth, thin metal tube and the bore has no rifling. The weapon is employed at short range (up to 1.5 meters).

Prior to firing, the pen body (the barrel of the weapon) is removed for loading and then replaced. To cock the weapon, the operating handle is pulled to the rear and turned left until it engages the safety lock. To fire, the weapon is pointed toward the target and the operating handle turned right. The operating handle disengages from the safety lock and pushes the firing pin forward, which strikes the primer by force of the spring.

Specifications:
Caliber .22 (5.6mm)
Overall length 126mm/4.96 inches

Length of barrel	65mm/2.56 inches
Outside diameter of barrel	12mm
Maximum effective range	1.5m/5 feet

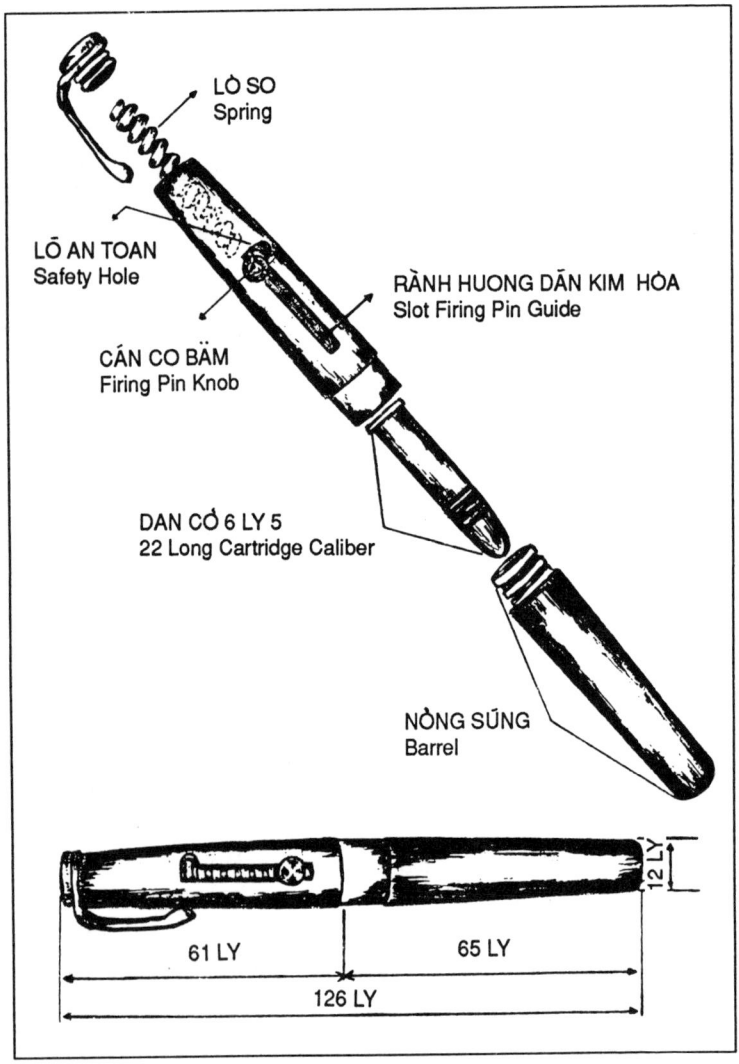

Viet Cong .22-caliber pen gun. (Illustration courtesy of ARVN headquarters)

CIA .22 LR Reloadable Stinger

The Stinger was issued concealed within a commercial squeeze tube. The weapon came with a spare barrel and eight rounds of ammunition packaged within a

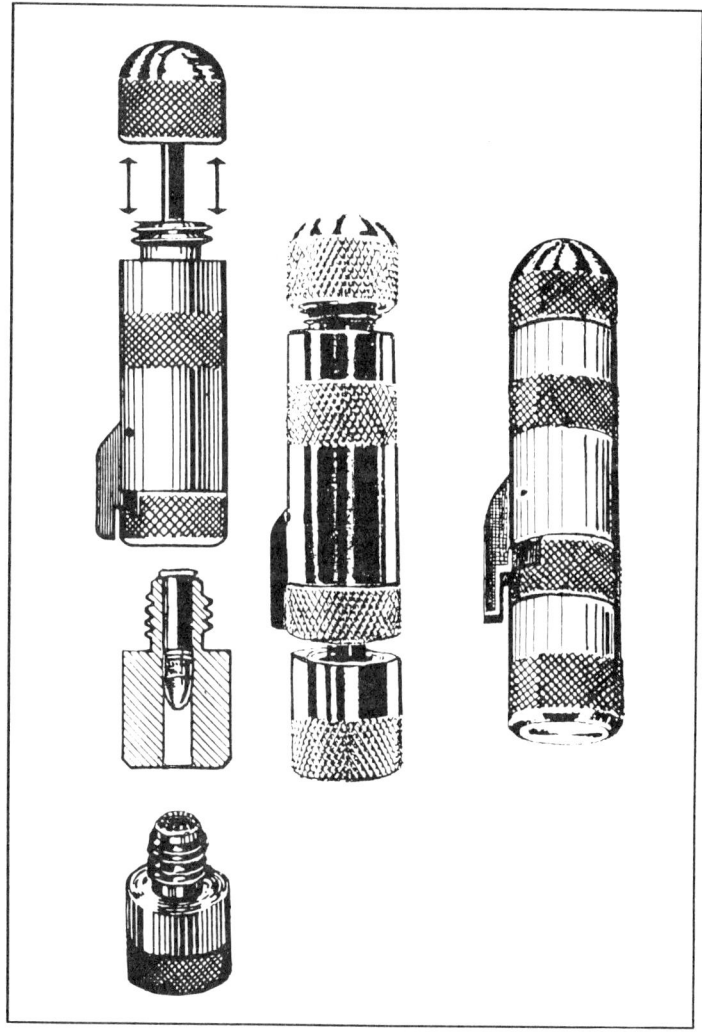

This CIA reloadable Stinger utilizes several features found in earlier designs. Note the absence of a muzzle exit. It has a bright machined-aluminum finish. (Author drawing)

clear plastic sleeve, which was fitted over the original barrel.

The barrels are unusual in that they are not bored all the way through but are reamed to within a tenth of an inch from the surface of what will become the muzzle upon firing. This serves a twofold purpose: it disguises the weapon in some of its applications and it keeps out foreign matter. It in no way affects the bullet upon exiting, as the range of this weapon is only ten feet. A blow-out plug may serve the same purpose.

Another feature of the barrel is that the chamber has a crenellated surface arranged about the circumference where the rim rests; this ensures that the rim is impinged from both sides when struck by the firing pin, which decreases the chance of a misfire. The operator is encouraged to practice with one barrel and save the other for active service. Although this weapon is single shot, it can be quickly reloaded if a loaded spare barrel is kept handy.

The Stinger is 3.250 inches long and 0.750 inches in diameter. It is made of machined aluminum and knurled deeply to provide grip surfaces for unscrewing the barrel for reloading and for gripping the end cap for recocking. The trigger is a press-down lever at the barrel end, and there is an Ailes-type safety ring. The pistol can be fired without undue discomfort to the hand, unlike smaller Stinger weapons. One Stinger model is entirely smooth and carried internally for maximum concealment. A lubricant gel is issued to aid concealment.

The CIA Stinger was closely copied by Military Armaments Corporation (MAC) and sold commercially as the Single Shot Survival Weapon. They are similar but not identical weapons. The barrel features of the Agency Stinger are not present on the MAC SSSW Stinger. The MAC version has an additional safety clip and minor differences in the finish and knurling patterns.

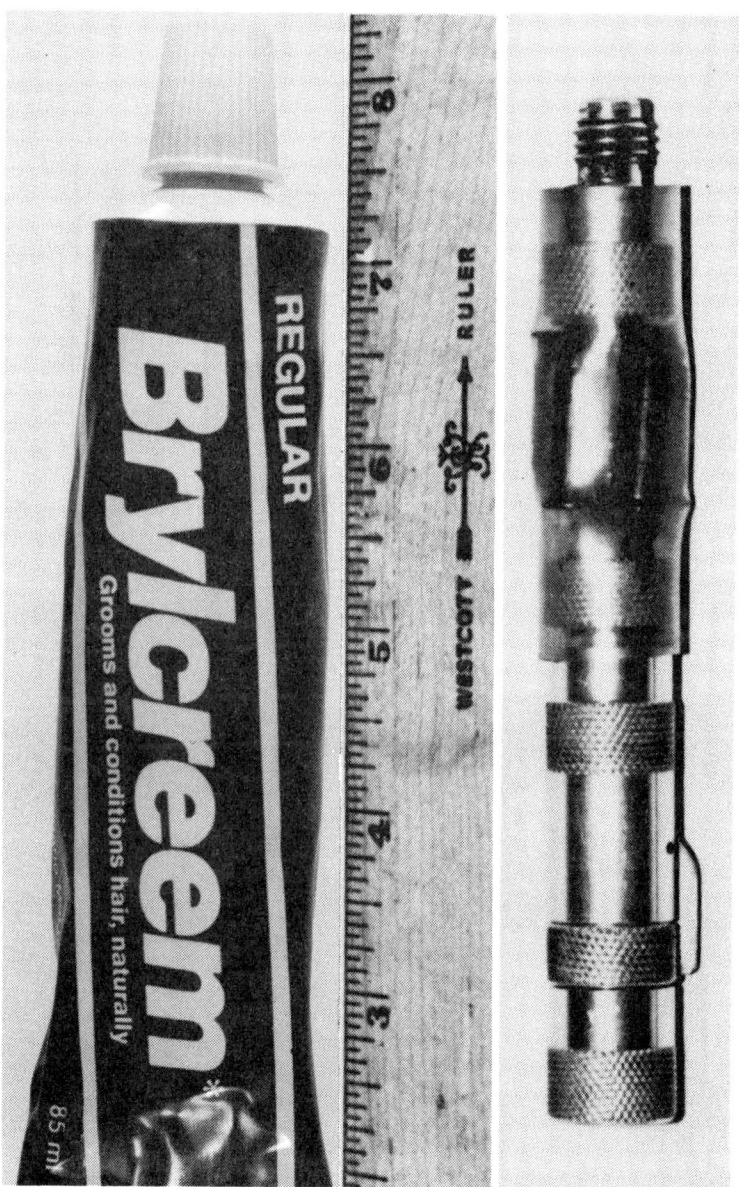

The CIA Stinger is disguised in a commercial squeeze tube. It comes complete with a spare practice barrel and eight rounds of ammo in a plastic sleeve. (Author photo)

CIA Stinger separated from packing sleeve. The spare barrel and ammo are still in the sleeve. (Photo courtesy of H. K. Melton, Clandestine Services Museum)

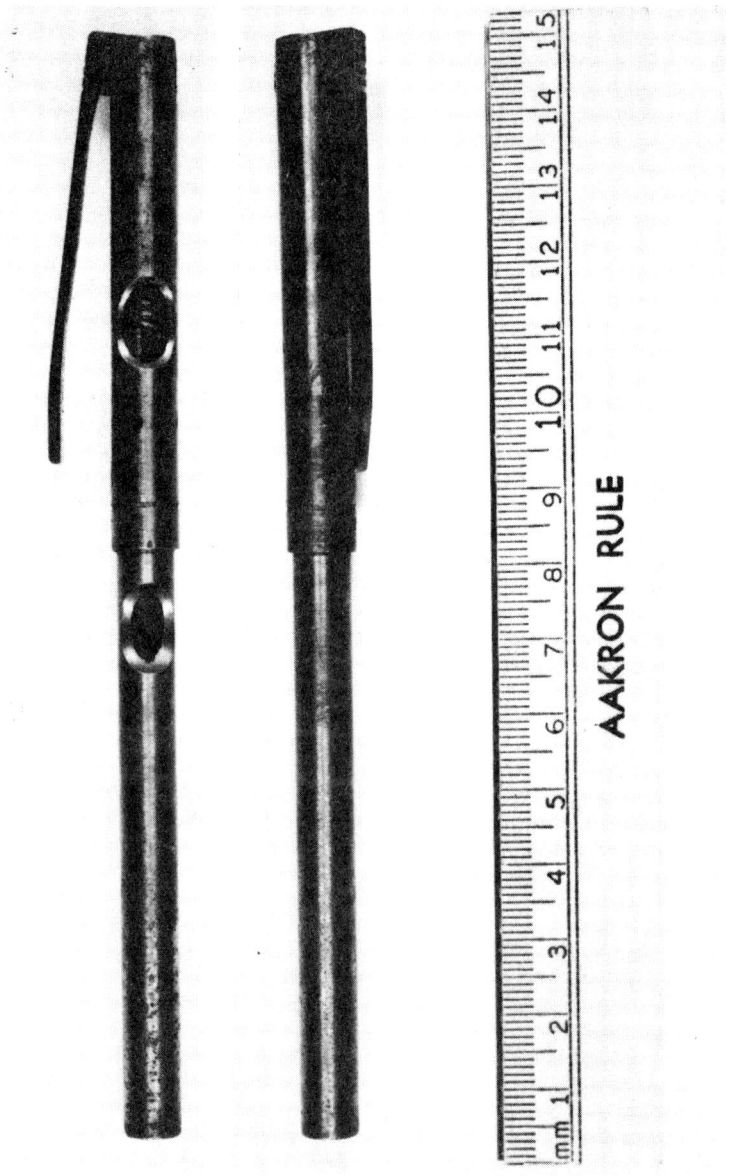

A nonreloadable .22-caliber British Secret Service Stinger. The cutaway at left shows a cocked demonstration device. The operations pen at right is fired. Pressing the pocket clip unhooks the firing pin. (Photo courtesy of H.K. Melton, Clandestine Services Museum)

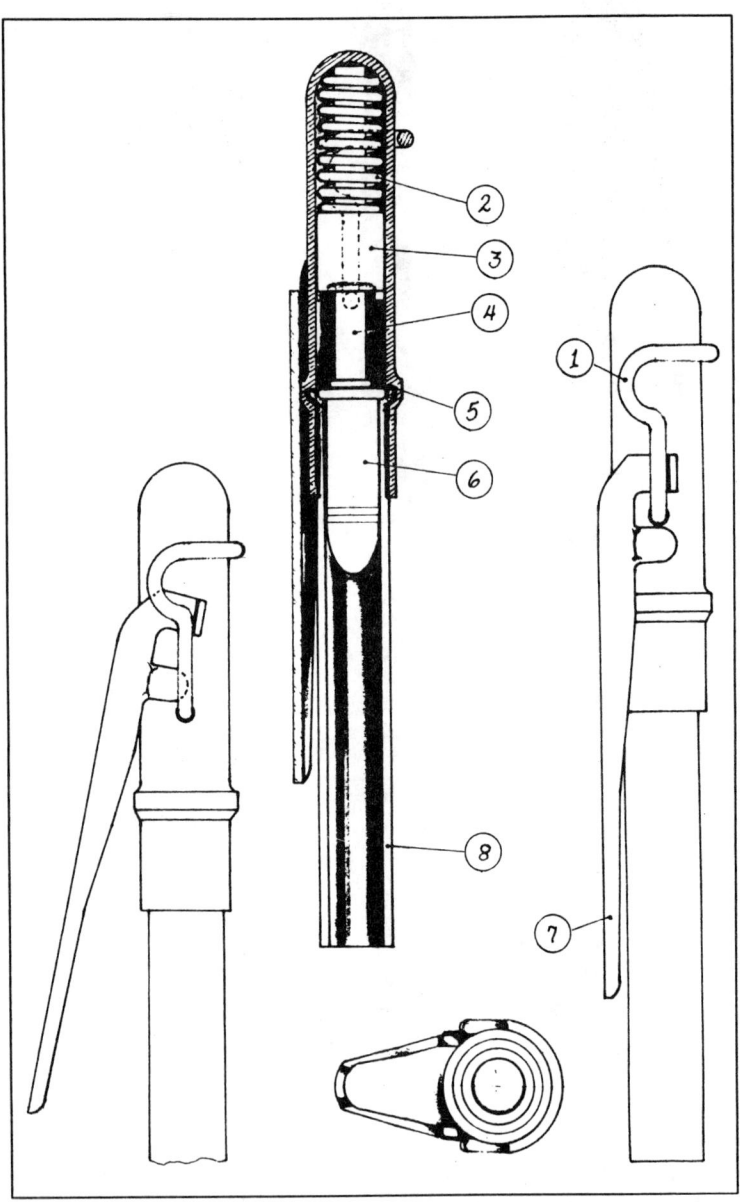

OSS .22 Stinger (T1). This cross-section drawing details the breech support rod and tubular firing pin. It is a precocked, nonreloadable item. (Illustration courtesy of Joe Ramos)

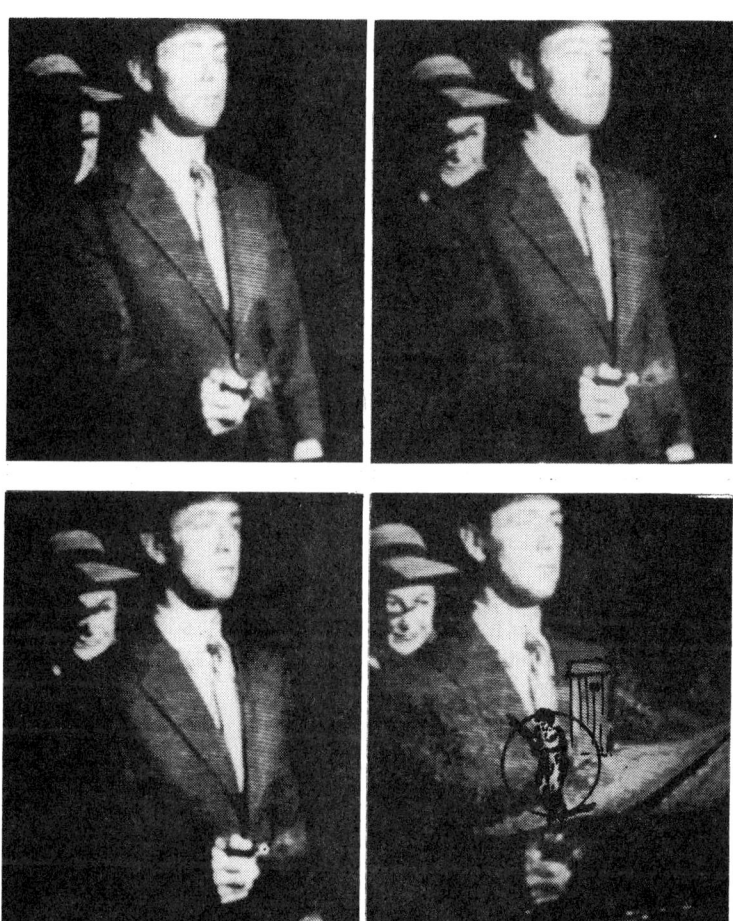

Alan Ladd shields Geraldine Fitzgerald while shooting a German railway sentry (circled, retouched to show scene shift) with a Stinger in this montage of stills from the movie *OSS*. (Photo courtesy of Display Ads/Paramount Studios)

Under the tutelage of Mitchell WerBell, MAC developed a silencer for their SSSW Stinger consisting of two end-cap wipe assemblies from their Ingram MAC-10 submachine gun. The tube, so I was told, was constructed from a can of baby food. With the silencer, the weapon was nearly always perceived as an assassina-

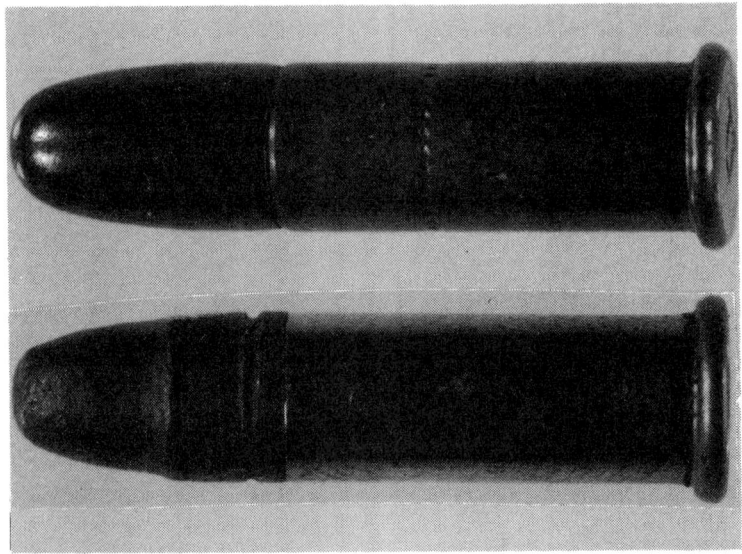

Special jacketed .22 bullet compared with a standard lead bullet underneath. The top bullet was used in Stingers, silenced pistols, survival rifles, and other weapons used by uniformed OSS agents. (Author photo)

tion device (similar to the British Welwand, a silenced En-Pen). Even the CIA Stinger was muffled, however, if the operator could maintain contact between muzzle and skin while shooting.

The Stinger's barrel is extremely short and the inaccuracy inherent in its design limits it to point-blank ranges. Muzzle velocity and penetration are also poor. Max Atchisson, the dean of American firearms innovators, designed a Stinger weapon while at MAC that had a barrel length nearly equal to the overall length of the weapon. He accomplished this by designing a U-shaped firing chamber, where the .22 round was fired in a reverse direction from the industrial blank that propelled it, the firing mechanism being parallel to and adjacent with the rifled bore. The weapon was highly concealable, yet it hit harder and

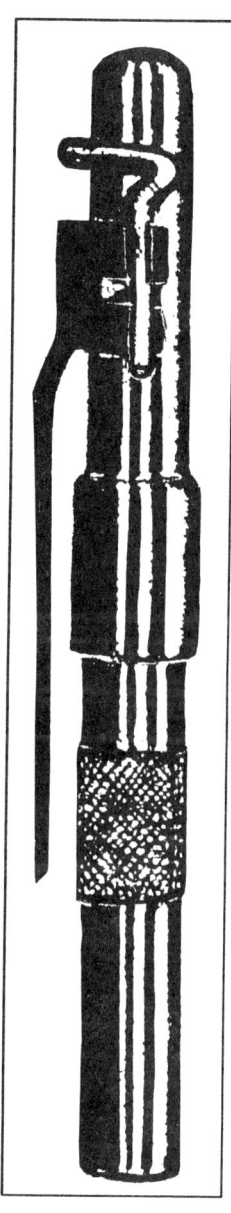

OSS .22 reloadable Stinger (fired). (Author drawing)

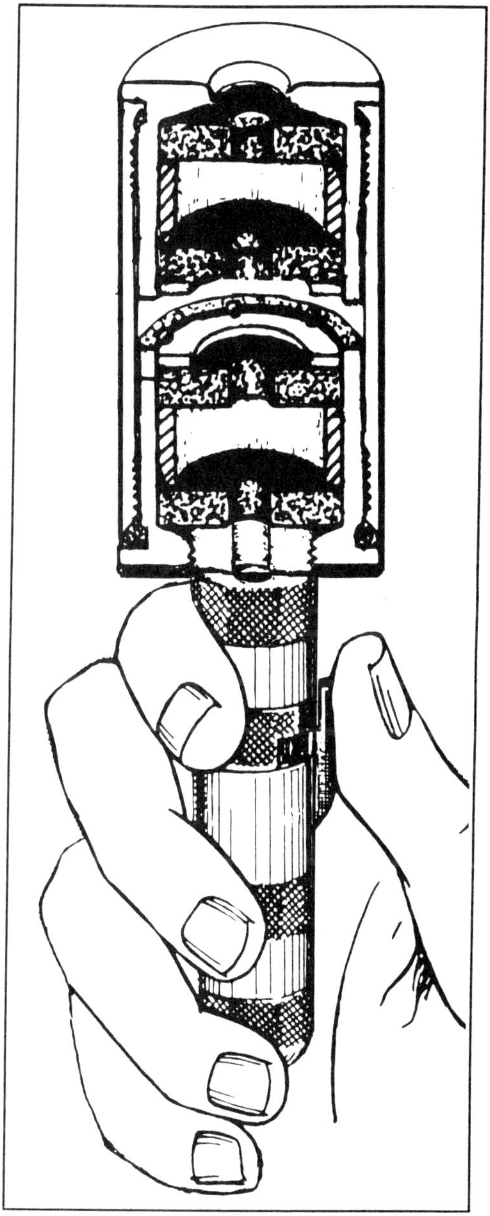

Military Armaments Corporation silenced Stinger. (Author drawing)

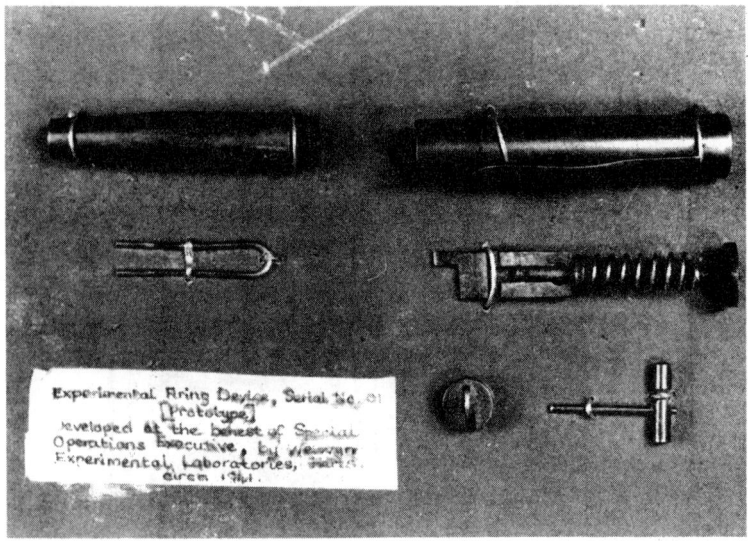

The SOE .22-caliber WELPEN showing arrangement of parts. Clockwise from bottom left: breech plug unscrewing wire spanner; barrel; receiver; cocking knob and firing pin; breech plug; trigger button. The trigger button has a cross-pin safety. (Photo courtesy of H.K. Melton, Clandestine Services Museum)

had longer range than other Stingers. Longer barrels could be manufactured for the CIA and MAC Stingers but such a modification would defeat their advantage of concealment.

CIA developed the Stinger for use in situations where only a weapon of maximum concealment could be employed. Places to hide the weapon require only a little imagination. It could be taped anywhere on the body—under the armpit, between the cheeks (the other cheeks), within a jockstrap holster, and so on.

CIA .22-caliber Camouflaged Weapons

These weapons were designed as escape and evasion aids. They are nonreloadable, single-shot, expendable-issue items. They can be concealed within pens, pencils, king-size cigarettes, wallets, or any personal

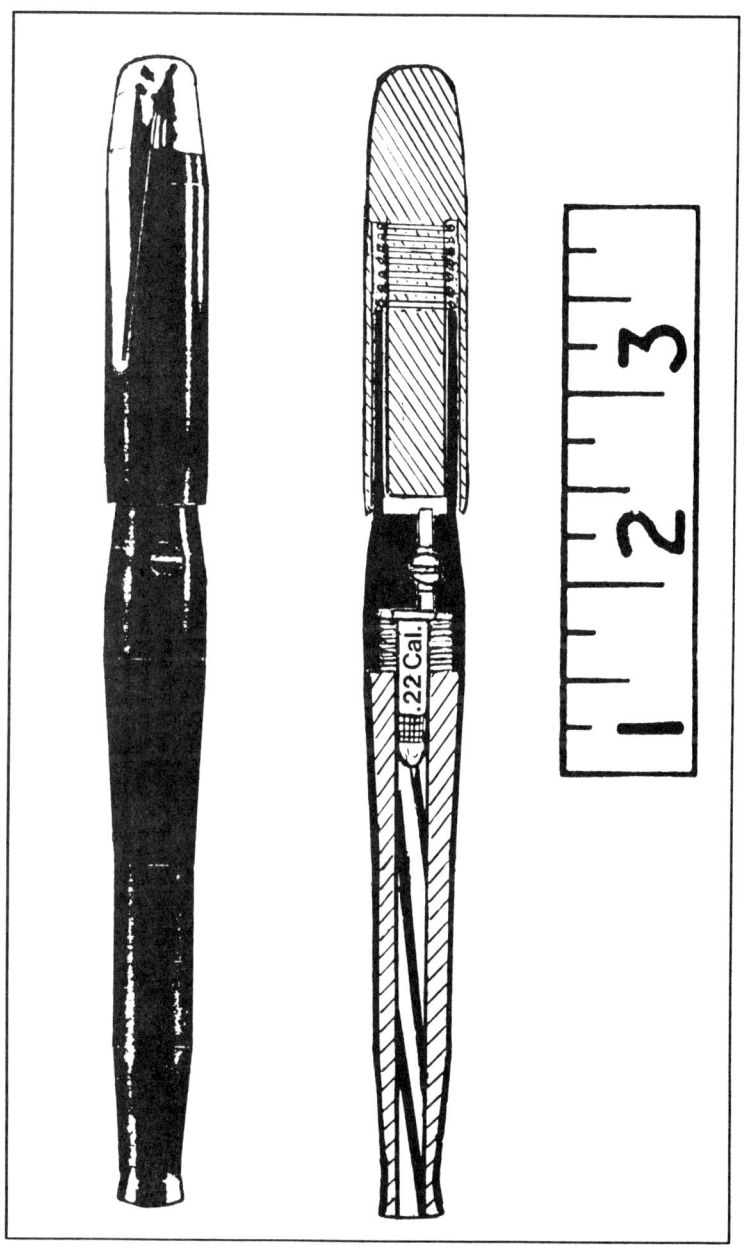

SOE .22-caliber slapfire pen gun. (Author drawing)

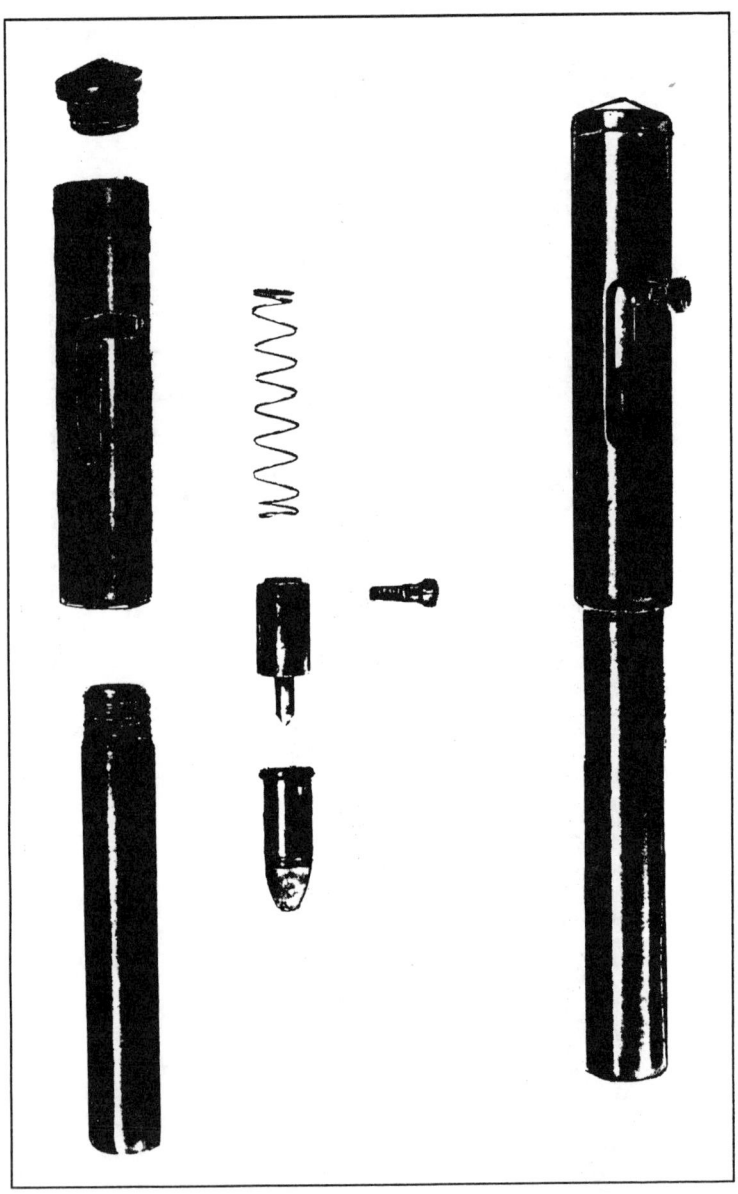

SOE .32-caliber pen gun. The basic design of this well-made, thick-walled pistol follows prewar tear gas pen guns. (Author photo)

Special Spy Weapons / 99

```
           AUXILIARY FIRING DEVICE
                  HAND HELD
                EN-PEN No1MK1
```

Description: An 0.22 Single-shot non-reloadable weapon, having a 3" barrel, and being 5" overall length. It has a completely fool-proof mechanism, a bolt being held captive by the displacement of two bearings. This is achieved by insertion of a 2" long rod which causes the bearings to move apart from the centre of the bolt in which they are concontained. The bearings move into small holes in the outer receiver walls, thus preventing the spring propelled bolt from moving ahead.

Attached to the rod is the pocket-clip which also doubles as the trigger. Movement of this approximately 3/4" to the rear will activate discharge.

When removed from its packing, a safety clip will be seen inserted through the receiver of the device. This must be removed just prior to issue; once this is done the pre-loaded item is live, and merely requires the clip to be slid to the rear.

To fire; The instructor must emphasis the correct modes of holding. Persons with small hands willfind the hand at side, actuating discharge with thumb on top satisfactory. The weapon may point ahead or to the rear. The En-Pen should be allowed to move freely in the hand, as owing to its small size and quite a smart recoil, it may not be grasped too strongly.

MAR.,1944

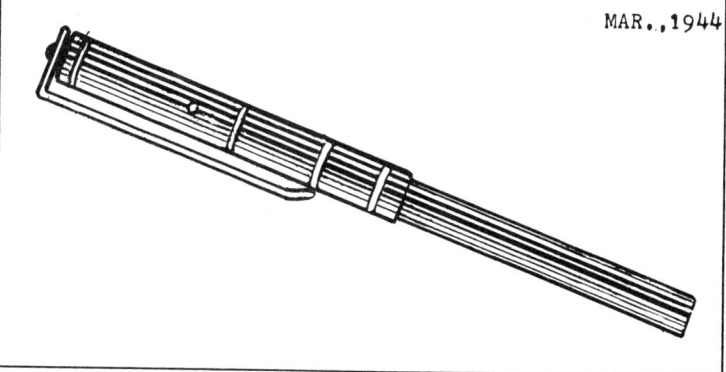

A sheet from a British Secret Service instruction manual on the En-Pen. (Document courtesy of H.K. Melton, Clandestine Services Museum)

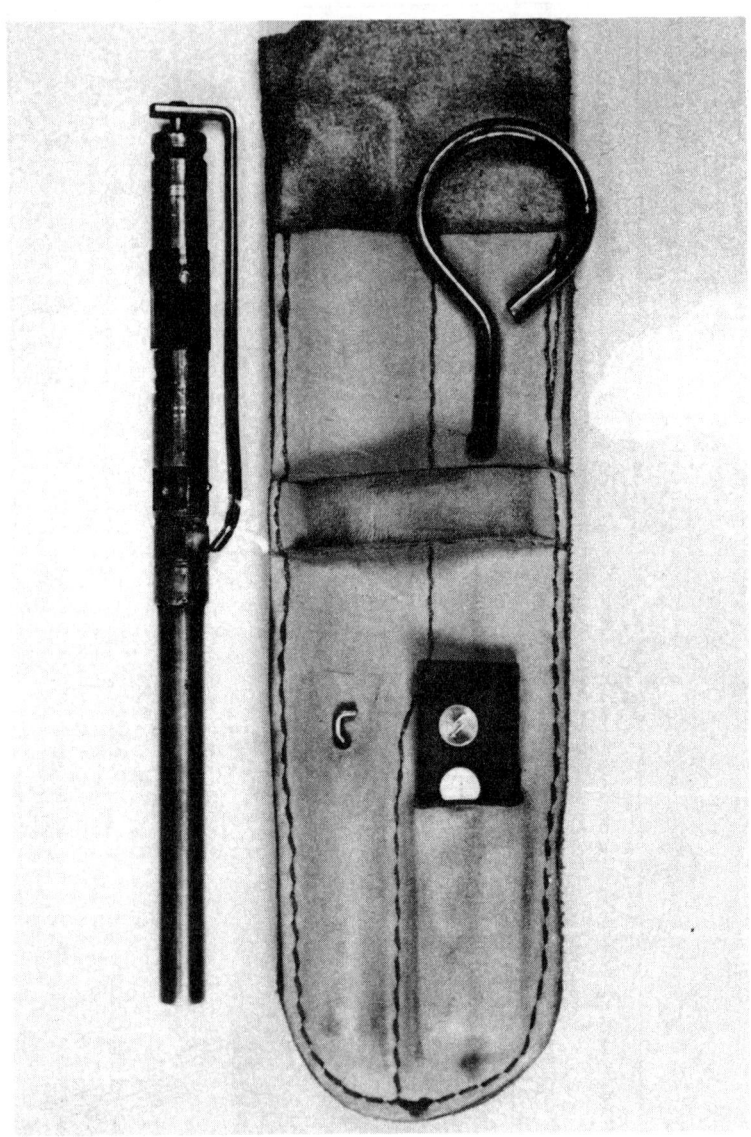

British Secret Service instructor's reloadable En-Pen with wallet holster and cleaning and cocking rod. Spare blanks are kept on a leather strip. (Photo courtesy of H.K. Melton, Clandestine Services Museum)

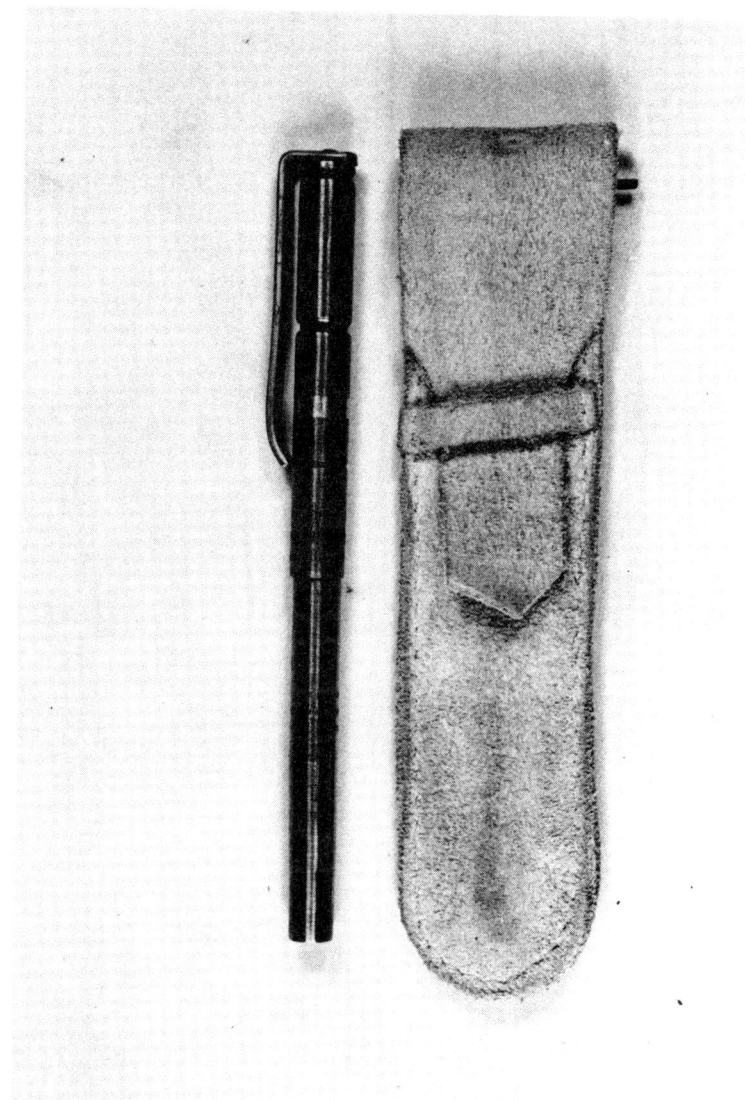

Operations En-Pen with homemade leather holster. This pen is not reloadable. A safety wire blocks the firing pin and winds around the deep groove at the midpoint under the pocket clip. (Photo courtesy of H.K. Melton, Clandestine Services Museum)

The .22-caliber SOE Welwand silenced En-Pen with extended pocket clip (trigger) and elasticized strap for shoulder rigging. (Photo courtesy of H. K. Melton, Clandestine Services Museum)

item supplied by the employee.

It should be noted that the muzzle energy of the longer-barreled weapons is greater, yet so is the recoil. Shot placement is vital; these weapons are lethal, but since there is but one round to fire, it must be true.

To fire one of these pen guns, the weapon is positioned in the hand as shown in the illustration. The safety device is removed by pulling the pin near the eraser cup. The gun is armed by turning the eraser cup counterclockwise until it stops. To fire, the user pushes forward with thumb and forefinger, allowing the weapon to recoil out of the hand upon discharge.

Specifications:

Caliber	.22
Bullet weight	40 grain
Bull's-eye powders	50 milligrams (short barrel)
	70 milligrams (longer barrels)
Barrel length	1.250 inches (pencil or Gaulois cigarette)
	3.000 inches (pen)
	5.000 inches (wallet, etc.)
Overall lengths	2.750 inches; 4.750 inches; 5.000+ in. (varies)
Muzzle velocity	760 feet per second (short barrel)
Penetration	1.750 inches (soft pine)
Range	0 - 10 feet
Safety	Pull wire or small pin

Quiet Special Purpose Pen Gun

This unique weapon fires a .22-caliber projectile pushed by an aluminum rod extruded by a short-stroke piston, which retains all the discharged gases from

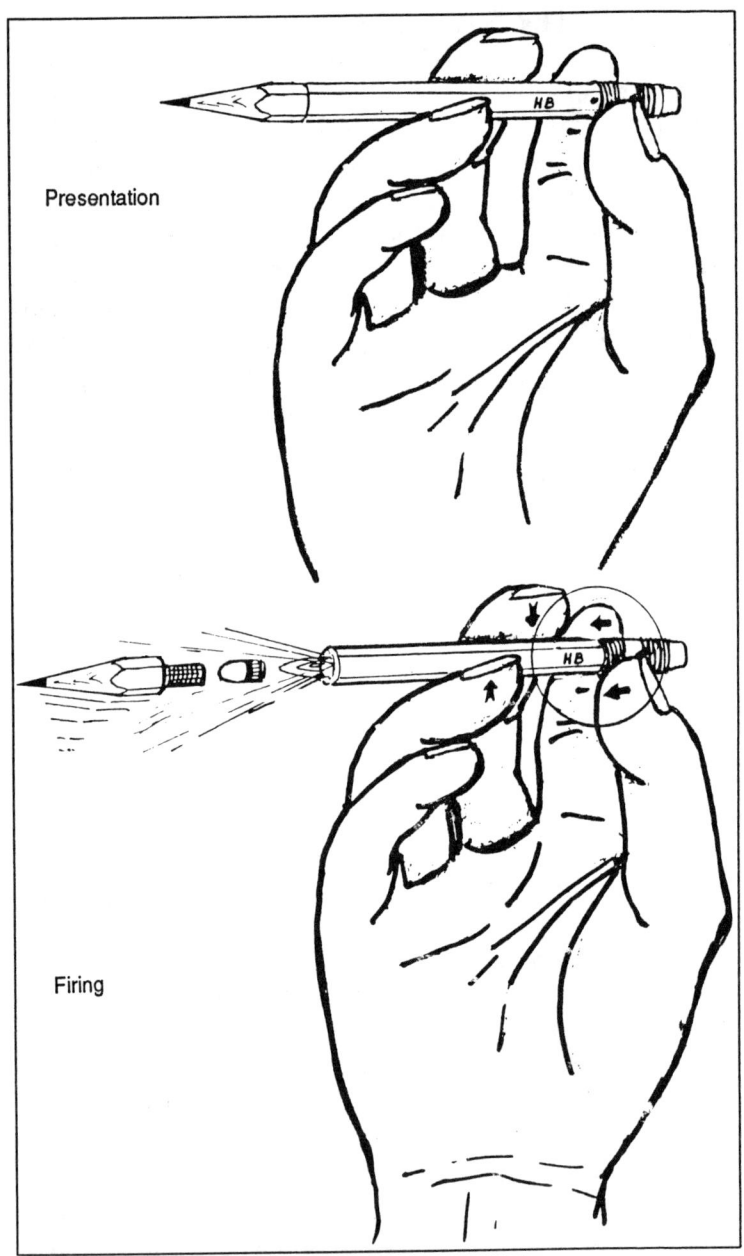

CIA E&E pencil pistol, model number 2. (Author drawing)

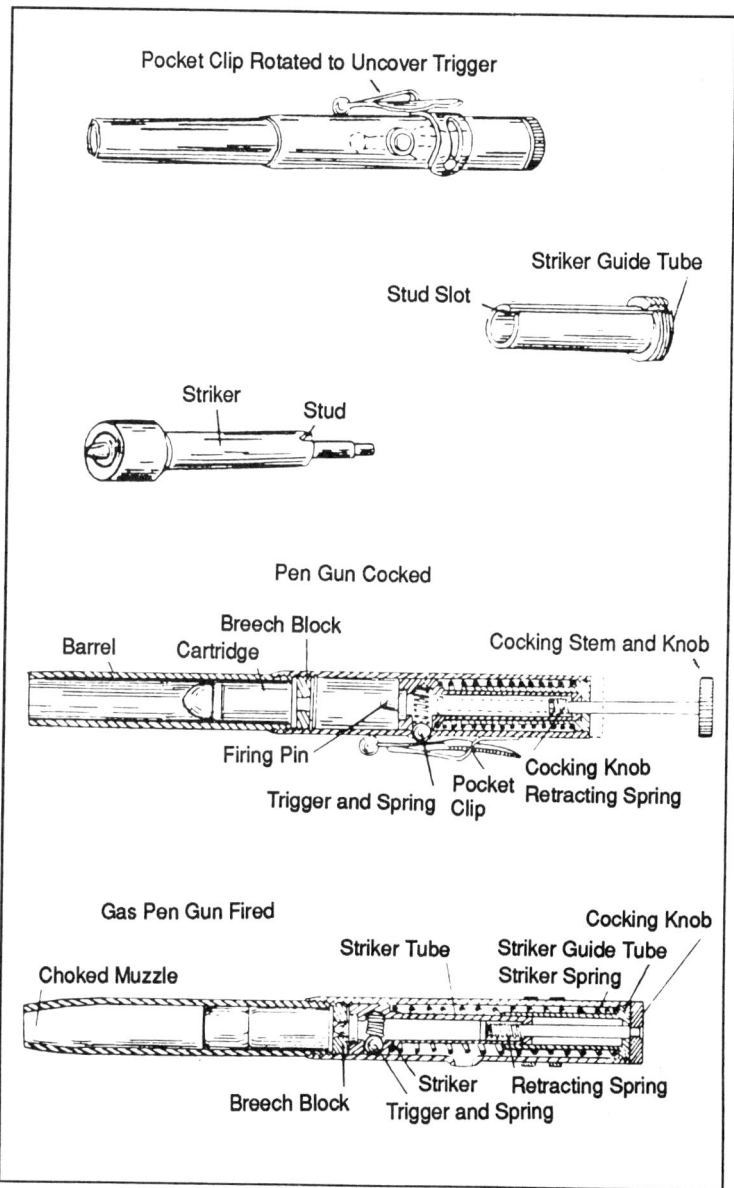

The Abbot pen gun issued by OSS fired gas as well as bullets. It is similar to but better made than the British WELPEN. (Illustration courtesy of Tom Swearengen)

ignition of the powder charge. The design has been purposely overbuilt since it doesn't rely on anything but thickness for strength; there are neither exotic alloys nor demanding manufacturing processes incorporated. It is a one-shot weapon and not readily reloadable in the field.

The loading process is quite involved. First, an engraved bullet needs to be made. This is accomplished by taking a #4B lead shot and forcing it down the muzzle with a loading rod until it exits at the breech. The process elongates the bullet and flattens the end being pressed through the rifling. The bullet, now pre-engraved, is inverted and reintroduced rounded-end first into the rifling at the breech. Spare bullets should be made for backup.

The next step is to place a small pistol primer in a steel receptacle at the rear of the piston housing, which is threaded to accept the firing-pin striker assembly. After the primer is seated (no tool is required), the striker assembly is screwed on.

The piston housing is prepared by emptying a .22 LR cartridge case full of gunpowder into it, topped by a tuft of wadded facial tissue tamped down by the large section of the piston. With the piston seated in that spot, the barrel, with the bullet engaged in the rifling, is screwed onto the housing.

The weapon is cocked by drawing back a split ring attached to the striker. The striker is notched to accept the engaging nose of the pivoting lever release that lies along the side of the unit.

To fire, merely aim and squeeze the lever. There will be no perceived sound from the weapon. The force generated within the chamber drives the piston forward against the barrel section. Its energy is transferred to the bullet. The piston will separate from the rod where they connect and the rod will fall to the ground a short distance from the muzzle. The round hits very hard since it is propelled by a larger charge than a regular .22 bullet. Duplex—even triplex—loads are options if more hitting weight is desired.

CIA Dart Gun

This device stands alone as a milestone in the development of clandestine weaponry. It represents a culmination of years of research toward finding a delivery system that would down man or beast, yet allow subsequent revival if deemed expedient. It incarnates the dart guns often pictured in films but which hitherto were not available in the real world. Its potential had never been realized when it was shown to the world in its pistol form during the Senate Select Committee on Assassinations Hearings.

The core of the system is the dart itself. It is a mass-stabilized, or javelin-type, projectile. It is balanced in flight by neither fins nor rotation but by virtue of its length over diameter ratio, with the center of gravity at three-fourths the distance from the tail end. The front end is made of heavy metal particles (steel or tungsten)—the tranquilizer Etorphin or M-99 is bonded within the tip with a blood/water-soluble bonding agent. The dart fits socket fashion into a magnesium or Teflon tail. Even if loaded backwards, it will right itself and assume a point-forward position in flight.

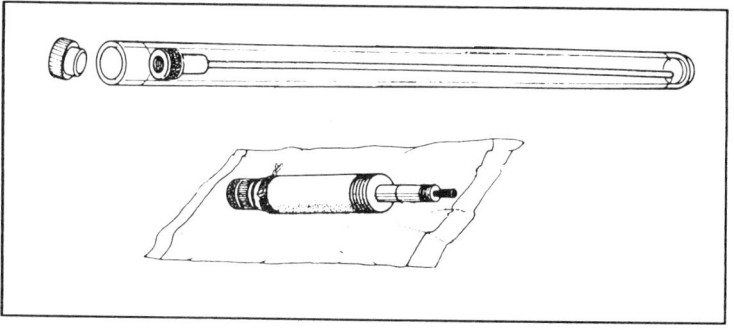

CIA dart gun ready for operations. (Author drawing)

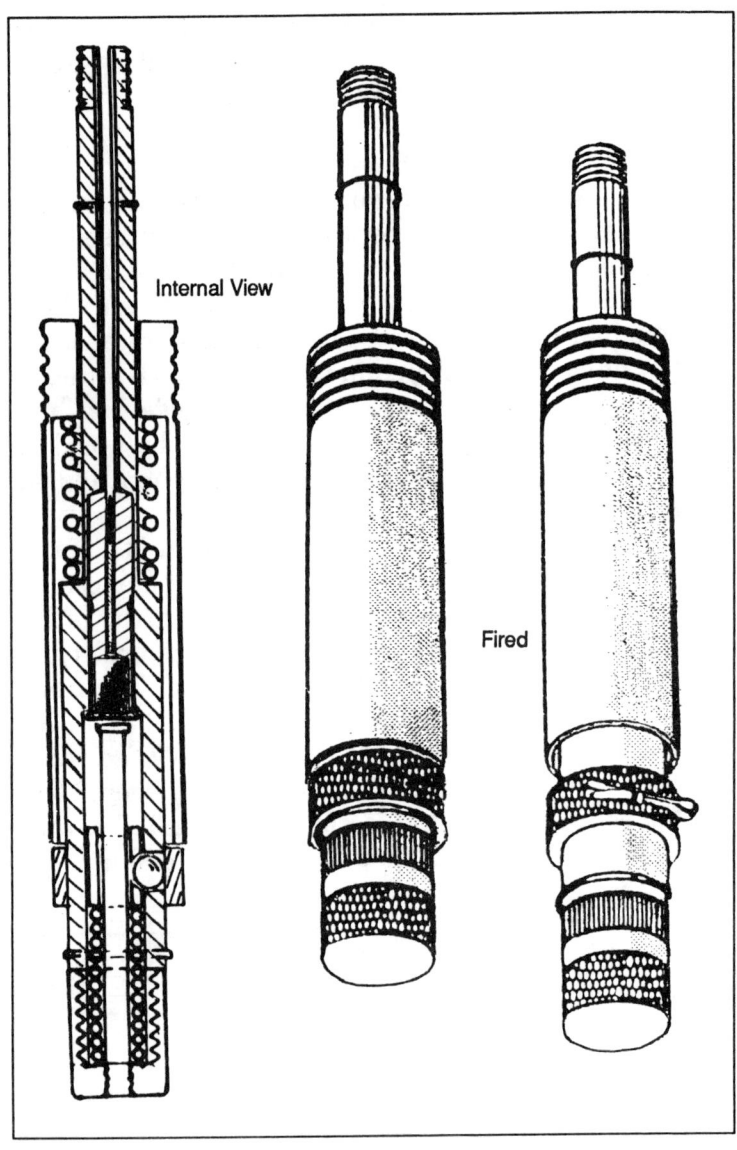

CIA dart gun in short-barrel configuration. Note cotter pin in safety ring in the illustration at right. Sliding the safety ring back will allow the ball bearing to pop into the thimble gap, allowing the hollow striker to move forward and fire the weapon. (Author drawing)

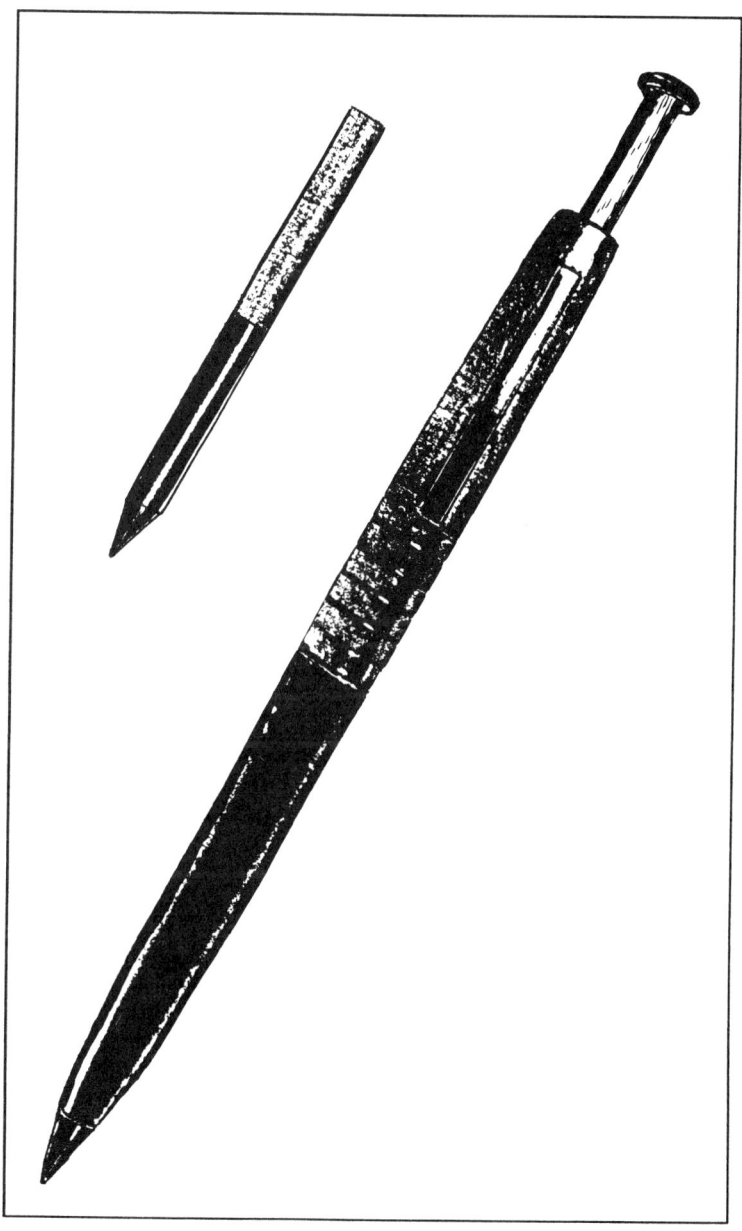

This Swiss dart gun fires a javelin-stabilized round by depressing the pocket clip, which sets off a .22 blank.

Aiming and firing the dart gun with barrel extension attached. The user must be careful not to bend or deflect the extension. (Author drawing)

The enlarged drawings of the cartridge case illustrate that it is a highly modified .22-caliber round. An adapter is crimped into the casing and remains within it during firing. The dart is contained within this adapter, which is lined with hypodermic-needle tubing. This tubing continues as the barrel liner of the pen gun and in the long-range extension. The dart is prevented from slipping from the adapter liner during transport by a grease dab.

Since the dart flies at such a high speed and has such a tiny diameter, it enters the target below the pain threshold, usually going unperceived unless mistaken for a mosquito bite. An accidental discharge during the development of the round confirms this fact. A researcher was shot with the dart, but the superficial wound was difficult to notice.

The projectile dissolves if left in the body and appears as a suspended, unidentifiable particle on X-ray. The Etorphin tranquilizer is most powerful and will take effect in a quarter to a half an hour. The subject will at first be unaware of his surroundings and will then fall asleep for six to eight hours. Grogginess is the only symptom noted during recovery. If the subject is to be revived after a shorter interval, the antidote is five milligrams of Nalorphine Hydrochloride administered intramuscularly by Syrette.

The subject must be protected from cold-weather exposure during the drugged state if his survival is essential to maintaining secrecy. Follow-up shots with the dart can be lethal. Etorphin is used on big African game, so it must be scaled accordingly when used against guard dogs, sentries, and the like.

The CIA dart gun utilizes a squeezer. To fire, the user must remove the safety cotter pin and barrel plug, affix the extension if needed (being careful not to bend it), take aim, and retract the thimble, which forces the safety ring back, firing the gun. It may be fired concealed within the hand by retracting the thimble with thumb and forefinger. The device should be preloaded, and it cannot be easily reloaded in the field. Since there is only one shot, the user must be aware that crosswinds can affect the dart's flight. The unit should therefore be tested under all conditions and scenarios in advance, including testing the darts on stray dogs.

Though the weapon makes very little noise upon discharge, small integral silencers can be fitted that hold the gases generated by the burning of the propellant powders to one overpressure or less.

APPENDIX

INVENTIONS RELATING TO PEN WEAPONS

George Webber; Chicago, Illinois; May 2, 1905; Patent #788,866; squeezer pistol.

Sergio M. Biason; Santa Barbara, Philippines; May 23, 1926; Patent #1,608,359; pen gun.

Dr. Byron C. Goss; Cleveland, Ohio; June 15, 1926; Patent #1,663,834, gas pen.

Scott M. Abbot; June 23, 1928; Patent #1,772,656; gas pen.

Frederick S. Cocho; Columbus, Ohio; August 21, 1928; Patent #1,681,172; pen gun.

William S. Darley; Chicago, Illinois; February 4, 1929; Patent #1,772,070; gas pen.

Peter Von Frantzius; Chicago, Illinois; September 9, 1930; Patent #1,775,178; gas pen.

Wallace M. Minto; Jersey City, New Jersey; October 6, 1931; Patent #1,826,562; gas pen.

Adrian S. Ailes; Cleveland, Ohio; February 21, 1933; Patent #1,897,992; gas billy.

Peter Von Frantzius; Chicago, Illinois; August 21, 1934; Patent #1,970,719; desk gun.

Merle A. Gill; Kansas City, Missouri; June 2, 1936;

Patent #2,042,934; squeezer pistol.

Don C. Williams; Huntington Park, California; August 7, 1956; Patent #2,757,474; gas pen.

Peter Von Frantzius; Chicago, Illinois; April 7, 1959; Patent #2,880,543; gas pen.

Russell O. Stefan, et al; Downey, California; July 17, 1962; Patent #3,044,360; pen flaregun.

Russell O. Stefan, et al; Downey, California; September 3, 1963; Patent #3,102,477; rocket flare.

Austin M. Wortley, Jr., et al; Devon, Pennsylvania; August 24, 1965; Patent #3,202,099; flaregun.

William H. Hiser; Decauter, Illinois; February 1, 1966; Patent #203,599; gas pens.

Austin M. Wortley, Jr.; Devon, Pennsylvania; March 8, 1966; Patent #203,996; gas pens.

Robert C. Mawhinney, et al; Castro Valley, California; October 3, 1967; Patent #3,344,711; dart.